Routledge Revivals

Industrial Technological Development

Technical innovation in industry is regarded by many people as the best way of making industry more profitable. A great deal of energy and time is being expended by businessmen and by governments discussing how best to bring about technical innovation. This book, which was first published in 1987, argues that all concerned with technical innovation should bear in mind the importance of 'networks'. 'Networks' are defined as the web of contacts which exist between suppliers, customers, and producers in industry. Drawing on extensive original research, the book discusses the need for co-ordinating technical research and development with suppliers and customers and examines in detail how this should best be done. This book is ideal for students of business and economics.

Industrial Technological Development
A Network Approach

Edited by
Håkan Håkansson

Routledge
Taylor & Francis Group

First published in 1987
by Croom Helm Ltd

This edition first published in 2015 by Routledge
2 Park Square, Milton Park, Abingdon, Oxon, OX14 4RN
and by Routledge
711 Third Avenue, New York, NY 10017

Routledge is an imprint of the Taylor & Francis Group, an informa business

Publisher's Note
The publisher has gone to great lengths to ensure the quality of this reprint but
points out that some imperfections in the original copies may be apparent.

Disclaimer
The publisher has made every effort to trace copyright holders and welcomes
correspondence from those they have been unable to contact.

A Library of Congress record exists under LC control number: 86013452

ISBN 13: 978-1-138-85016-3 (hbk)
ISBN 13: 978-1-315-72493-5 (ebk)

INDUSTRIAL TECHNOLOGICAL DEVELOPMENT

A Network Approach

Edited by

HÅKAN HÅKANSSON

CROOM HELM
London • Sydney • Dover, New Hampshire

© 1987 Håkan Håkansson
Croom Helm Ltd, Provident House, Burrell Row,
Beckenham, Kent, BR3 1AT
Croom Helm Australia Pty Ltd, Suite 4, 6th Floor,
64-76 Kippax Street, Surry Hills, NSW 2010, Australia

British Library Cataloguing in Publication Data
Industrial technological development: a
    network approach.
    1. Technological innovations
    I. Håkansson, Håkan
    338'.06   HD45
    ISBN 0-7099-3763-6

Croom Helm, 27 South Main Street,
Wolfeboro, New Hampshire 03894-2069, USA

Library of Congress Cataloging-in-Publication Data
Industrial technological development.

    Bibliography: p.
    1. Technological innovations. 2. Research,
Industrial. 3. Cooperation. I. Håkansson, Håkan,
1947-
T173.153   1986   607'.2   86-13452
ISBN 0-7099-3763-6

Printed and bound in Great Britain
by Billing & Sons Limited, Worcester.

CONTENTS

Chapter Three

PRODUCT DEVELOPMENT IN NETWORKS
by Håkan Håkansson 84

Chapter Four

SUPPLIER MANAGEMENT AND TECHNOLOGICAL
DEVELOPMENT
by Björn Axelsson 128

Chapter Five

TECHNOLOGICAL DEVELOPMENT AND THE
INDIVIDUAL'S CONTACT NETWORK
by Cecilia Hamfelt and Ann–Kristin Lindberg 177

Chapter Six

STRATEGIC IMPLICATIONS

References

Preface

A 19th century Swedish poet, Ola Hansson, concluded one of his essays with the following melancholy reflection: *And while the twilight thickened and the countryside fell quietly to sleep in the hues, I thought of the many melodies which life never awakens.* In a similar manner, technological development is described in this book as a process wherein certain ideas come to life while others remain hidden, perhaps forever. An important and fundamental precept in our work has been that we consider technological development as being the result of the interaction between different corporations, organizations and individuals instead of being the consequence of one individual actor's performance. This is, however, not a random process. On the contrary, technological development is here considered to be an integrated part of the structure from which it arises and which it as a rule helps to develop and improve. We shall never know which innovations other structures have brought to life. Like the Swedish poet, we can just reflect over the possibilities.

We use a network approach as a way of understanding technological development. In the same way, there is quite naturally a network behind the writing of this book. First of all, we would like to thank the informal research team of which we are members, with special appreciation going to Elisabeth Brandel (University of Uppsala), David Ford (University of Bath), Jan Johanson (University of Uppsala), Anders Lundgren and Lars-Gunnar Mattsson (Stockholm School of Economics), Ivan Snehota (University of Bocconi), Peter W Turnbull (University of Manchester, Institute for Science and Technology), Alexandra Waluszewski and Björn Wootz (University of Uppsala).

We are also deeply grateful to the representatives of various industrial companies who in volunteering their precious time made it possible for us to gather detailed and exact descriptions of the actual development process.

Chapters 4 and 5 were translated from the Swedish by Marko Modiano B.A., who also proofread Chapters 1, 3 and 6. Jean Gray contributed by proofreading Chapter 2.

Inger Håkansson did the typing and the technical work which made computer transfer possible. The figures and tables were

1

designed by Karin Johansson. Economic support was provided by the Swedish Council for Research in Humanities and Social Sciences, the Swedish National Board for Technical Development, Handelsbanken's Research Foundation, the Marketing Technology Center and the University of Uppsala.

Uppsala December 1985

Håkan Håkansson

Chapter One

INTRODUCTION

Technological Innovation through Interaction

The dominant perspective concerning technical development can very much be characterized as the Newton syndrome. According to the legend Newton got his idea which led to the theory of gravitation when he was lying under an apple tree watching an apple falling. The lonely innovator and the flash of genius has since then characterized our way of looking at knowledge development and thereby also at technical development. The existence of for example the Noble prize is an excellent illustration of this perspective. The existence of highly complex and sophisticated equipment in research has only changed the picture a little. The lonely innovator is not lying under a tree anymore, instead he or she is working late in the evening in the high-technology laboratory.

This view of knowledge and technical development has also affected the approach at the company level[1], where product development is seen as an internal problem. The company is advised to design a systematic product development process in order to develop the 'right products'. Products should be developed within the company and then be introduced to the market.[2]

Our view is quite different. An important part of the development process, we suggest, takes place in the form of a technical exchange between different 'actors' such as individuals or companies. Accordingly, interest should be focused as much on the interaction between different actors as on what happens within the actors. An innovation, therefore, should not be seen as the product of only one actor but as the result of an interplay between two or more actors; in other words as a product of a 'network' of actors. At least, this is our conclusion in regard to the company level which is the focus of this book. The conclusion is based upon three main arguments related to knowledge development, resource mobilization, and resource coordination respectively, and each of these factors will now be explained.

3

Knowledge development

New knowledge in terms of new product or process ideas often emerges at the interface between different knowledge areas. In exchange situations different kinds of knowledge come together (are combined or confronted) to create innovative situations. Technical solutions developed for other situations by one of the actors can be useful to the other. Thus, by combining experience, new ideas can emerge. A special case is when the exchange takes place between a buyer and a seller. It means that the needs of the buyer are confronted with the possible technical solutions known by the seller. This provides an opportunity to revise and redefine both the needs and the solutions and in this way find new possibilities.

There are two reasons for the positive effects on the innovation process of the bringing together of different 'knowledge bodies'. The first one was described above and can be called the interactive effect. The second one is related to the fact that new products are often based on the combination of several technologies. Thus, there is a need for competence from several technological areas. An exchange situation can help to create an interface between different specialists, thus producing a multi-competence effect.

Obviously however, all exchange situations do not necessarily produce innovation. Innovations will only occur where certain conditions exist and these will be explored later on.

Resource mobilization

An invention in the form of a theoretical model or formula can be seen in isolation. But as soon as it materializes in the form of a product, system, or service it becomes dependent on other products, systems, and services. There are also similar dependencies between the invention and the actors involved as the latter have to learn how to use the invention and how to combine it with other products. This means that the actors have to adapt to a larger or lesser degree in order to make use of the invention and turn it into an innovation. It also means that the innovation has to be adapted, revised, and redesigned in order to become useful in different situations. The innovation process, thus, has elements of learning, adaptation, and socialization. All these elements

4

require resources, usually in an environment where resources are scarce and where other activities compete for the same resources. Accordingly the innovation process can be compared to a mobilization process which in turn must be based on extensive interaction processes.

Resource coordination

As noted in the previous section, development resources within each company are normally limited. At the same time the total amount of knowledge has increased enormously over the last twenty years and continues to increase at a growing rate. The only way for the individual company to handle this problem has been to specialize its development resources in certain limited areas. An R&D manager for an advanced electronic company put it as follows: *It is stupid to try to develop products by yourself that can be much more effectively developed by a supplier.*

This specialization process follows   side by side with the increased specialization in production facilities. The result is a large number of small, highly specialized development units which increasingly need to be coordinated. This coordination is handled through a series of exchange relationships linking all these units together.

Cooperation between companies

The above three arguments can be seen as major reasons why a company may consider technical cooperation as a suitable and in some circumstances the only possible opportunity for technological development. By doing so the company can attain one or both of the interactive and multicompetence effects of knowledge development. Cooperation is also a way to mobilize external resources. For example, by engaging a large customer in the development of a new product that customer will at a later stage certainly be much more positive and willing to try or test the final product. Similarly, the company can obtain positive effects in several ways by coordinating its development activities with those of suppliers, customers, and producers of complementary products.

However, cooperation may also create problems. Some of these are connected with the increased complexity of handling the development process when several actors are involved. How-

5

ever, the most important problem is of a political nature. The company has to handle relationships involving both cooperative and conflicting elements. That means that each relationship must be handled in a sensitive and diplomatic way. Furthermore, there are also interdependencies between the relationships. By working together with certain counterparts others may feel rejected or at least less appreciated. In some situations these difficulties can be very serious and severely damage the whole development process. Nevertheless, they can be handled if the parties have the right features in terms of political judgement, diplomatic skills and social exchange abilities.

In this book many examples of cooperative technical development relationships will be described, demonstrating that there are a growing number of companies that already work in this way. At the same time we are convinced that at present only a small part of the potential combination possibilities are cultivated.

In order to give an illustration of different kinds of cooperations, their characteristics, the types of counterpart that are involved, how the development work is carried out etc, we shall now briefly describe some examples.

Examples of Technical Cooperation

It is possible to categorize technical cooperation in several ways. For example, they can be grouped in relation to the duration of the cooperation from short term project cooperation to life-long cooperations; to type of technical knowledge in terms of basic versus applied research; to degree of formalization; etc. However, we shall use a very simple grouping of three categories depending on type of counterpart. The first group can be called vertical cooperation and it includes all cooperation in seller-buyer relationships. The second group - horizontal competitive cooperation - includes cooperation between companies which basically are competitors. Lastly the third group - horizontal complementary cooperation - encompasses cases where the producers of complementary products cooperate.

There are often good reasons for both the selling and the buying company to develop technical cooperation. The seller can increase its knowledge about customer needs and develop both products and technical ability. The buying company can get products or services better fitted to its market or production requirements. Vertical cooperation can in this way affect the costs, the revenues and the profits of both the customer and the supplier. This type of cooperation is often of an informal character. It is part of an ongoing relationship. Futhermore, it can be permanent or last only as long as the current project. Some can be large and spectacular but usually they are smaller and of a day-to-day rationalization type. One spectacular example in Sweden has been the cooperation between the Ericsson Group and its customer the Swedish state owned telephone company Televerket in developing the AXE system. The project was organized as a jointly created company Ellemtel. It took more than 7 years and the R&D cost amounted to roughly 500 M Swedish crowns.

Horizontal competitive cooperations are usually of a quite different character. They are more formalized and project oriented and also more difficult to keep alive as there are no day-to-day activities connecting the companies. Some successful examples of this type are the cooperation between the airplane producers SAAB and Fairchild in developing and producing the aircraft Saab-Fairchild 340; between the car producers Volvo and Renault in designing and producing automotive components and between the German and Japanese photo companies - the cooperation between Zeiss and Yashica and Leitz and Minolta. All these cooperations basically try to take advantage of specialization and large scale effects in development and production. For example in the Saab-Fairchild case, Fairchild is responsible for manufacturing the wings, nacelles and tail section while Saab is responsible for the fuselage and final assembly. This type of cooperation also has important effects on the competition. The market becomes more 'structured'.

The third type of technical cooperation - the horizontal complementary type - is in some ways similar to both of the other types. The fact that the companies are complementary gives the same natural basis for cooperation as the buyer-seller relationship. On the other hand the lack of repetitive day-to-day contact makes this type similar to the competitive cooperation type.

The complementarity is often based on the fact that the cus-

7

tomer uses products from different suppliers together. A well-known example of this kind of cooperation in Sweden is between Sandvik and Atlas Copco. These companies launched together the 'Swedish method of mining' in the late 40s combining carbide drills from Sandvik with light drilling machines from Atlas Copco. Since then there has been continuous cooperation between these two companies. Other examples can be found in connection with system selling or large turn-key projects.

This type of cooperation is usually highly formalized and often related to a specific project, and occurs to solve a particular technical problem or to take advantage of a special opportunity. However, horizontal complementary cooperation can lead to establishment of technical and commercial day-to-day contacts between the companies, which in turn may lead to a much longer term relationship.

Thus, the lack of commercial day-to-day activities gives this type of cooperation specific difficulties. The worse is that companies may agree to and take part in the cooperation in order to, for example, protect themselves in respect to technical development without making any real effort to complete the project.

Relationships between Companies

An important starting point for this book is the earlier research on relationships between industrial goods companies such as studies of supplier-customer relationships and another comes from the more general studies of inter-organizational relationships (for summaries see Håkansson (ed., 1982), Turnbull & Valla (eds., 1985), Van de Ven et al. (1975), and Aldrich (1979)). The basic assumption is that there exist exchange relationships between organizational units, e.g. between selling and buying firms, and that these relationships create interdependencies between the units. Based on this assumption an interaction model for the analyses of industrial markets has been developed. This model, as described in Håkansson (ed., 1982), consists of four groups of variables:

1. The interaction process.
2. The participants in the interaction process.

8

3. The environment within which interaction takes place.
4. The atmosphere affecting and affected by the interaction.

Within the first variable group, one subgroup of variables is related to individual episodes describing short-term exchange of products, information, money and social symbols. The other subgroup is concerned with the long-term relationship in terms of adaptations, contact pattern and institutionalization.

The participants are characterized by their technologies, organizational features, and personnel. The importance of these characteristics is demonstrated by the fact that the interaction process in many industrial market situations can be seen as a means of linking different technological units to each other in an efficient way.

The interaction is not taking place in a vacuum but must be seen as a part of a wider environment which can be described in terms of structure, dynamism, internationalization and social system. These environmental variables belong to the third group.

The fourth variable group, the atmosphere, is dependent on the other three groups of variables. They can be seen as intervening variables which means that they are the mechanism by which the other variables are related to each other. The atmosphere is described in terms of power-dependence, state of conflict or cooperation, overall closeness or distance and the parties' mutual expectations.

The interaction model is a theoretical description of the development of relationships in industrial markets. Below we will give some empirical findings regarding these relationships.

Duration of relationships

Each relationship has a certain duration. The more important ones can be very long-lasting. In Table 1:1 the age-distribution for about 500 European seller-buyer relationships is given. The table indicates that long term relationships are especially common in the home market and for supplying countries that for a long time have been exporting a large share of their industrial production (Sweden and Germany).

This long term nature of relationships is important for several reasons. Firstly, it shows that the companies must in practice take future exchange probabilities into account. There is, therefore, a

Table 1:1   Age of Relationships between Buyers and Sellers in different
             Country Markets (in years).

Customer situated in	Supplier situated in				Weighted average
	France	Germany	Sweden	Britain	
France	21	10	10	3	8
Germany	7	15	20	6	11
Italy	7	12	20	7	12
Sweden	6	12	24	12	10
Britain	6	15	14	30	12
Weighted average	7	12	16	7	11

(Source: Hallén, 1985)

need for a long term perspective in the choice of suitable actions within the relationships. Secondly, it shows that there must be a degree of cooperation within the exchange. Thus there must be certain positive effects of being loyal and/or ways to handle conflicts other than by ending the relationship. Thirdly, the long duration indicates a certain strength of bond between the actors which in turn has a stabilizing effect. However, stability should not be confused with stagnation and low standards. There is always a certain degree of conflict within a relationship. But using Hirschmans (1970) concepts we can say that the two counterparts have learned to use voice instead of exit to solve conflicts.

Function of relationships

Relationships are one of the most valuable resources that a company possesses. They have been built up over a long period of time and a lot of manpower, travel expenses and other resources have been invested. In other words they are large and important investments that have to be taken care of and maintained in different ways.

These relationships (i.e. investments) are made by the company in order to serve certain functions. At least three main functions can be identified:

1.   To increase productivity or technical efficiency; the relationships often include adaptations of different kinds such as in products, production, deliveries, and storing. This

can reduce the total costs considerably - for example by lowering production costs, storing costs, and handling costs. The adaptations are of two kinds. Firstly there are larger adaptations made in the early stage of the relationships or when they are drastically changed. Secondly there are day-to-day rationalizations that go on more or less continuously.

2. To serve as information channels: The relationships provide important communication channels. The company needs accurate, detailed, and multifarious information. This information can only be obtained from actors that have the knowledge and are prepared to share it with others. The company also needs to have counterparts which in an active way supply the company with information as the latter in many situations does not know that a certain type of information exists. The company, thus, needs to obtain answers to its questions as well as to be continually informed about matters that are relevant to it. Both these activities require 'senders' or 'transmitters'. And the only way to solve this problem is to establish appropriate relationships.

3. To increase control (power); A wide network of relationships make the world a little more stable and controllable which is important to all involved. The relationships have in this way a power function. By building up relationships the company gets control in different ways - through information, through friendship, and through technical and other bonds to counterparts which interlock the various companies.

Relationships therefore serve important functions in terms of efficiency, stability and control. In this way they mainly serve as a conserving factor. But this is not at all the complete picture as the relationships can withold a dynamic feature. Relationships, even if they are very well established, always retain a feeling of freedom to each party which in turn give relationships a special tension. This tension drives the parties to continually develop the relationships and prevents them from becoming too institutionalized. The relationships should not, at least as we see them, be directly compared with hierarchical control or integration. A

Table 1:2   Social and Technical Content of Relationships.

a) Degree of closeness and openess

Scale	1	2	3	4	5
Percentage of relationships	13%	10%	38%	19%	20%

1 = Strict business relationships. No personal commitments.
5 = Close personal relationship. Open and cooperative atmosphere.

b) R&D personnel taking part

	Percentage of relationships
In the selling company	67%
In the buying company	46%

c) Production personnel taking part

	Percentage of the relationships
In the selling company	47%
In the buying company	70%

much better theoretical ground for comparisons is to see them as elements in loosely coupled systems (Weick, 1976).

An example illustrating the last point was given by a manager in Sala International - a Swedish producer of mining equipment.

We have always worked closely with the mining company Boliden. They have helped us in development work by testing, new equipment, discussing technical problems and needs, and so on. The whole relationship can be described as symbiotic. The only period when it did not work very well was the six years when Boliden owned us. Then, the question normally was: Why do you come here and disturb us? Mind your own business.

Our conclusion is obvious. The formal integration had taken away the tension and the two units did not find new cooperative forms.

Content of the relationships

The exchange within the relationships can be described in several dimensions. Two important ones from a technical development

12

point of view are the technical and social content. The technical content includes the exchange of technical information and knowledge as well as technical activities such as adaptations in the production process or the products. The social content consists of the exchange of social symbols, i.e. friendship, mutual trust and confidence. This is important as all exchange episodes include uncertainty. The social content is especially important when the exchange regards technical development.

In order to illustrate the importance and nature of the technical and social content of relationships we can show the results of an investigation of 37 relationships between Swedish special steel companies and their most important customers in Sweden, West Germany, Italy, France and the UK (Table 1:2). As the table shows, technical personnel are taking an active part - on at least one side - in about two thirds of the relationships. In about the same share there is a rather open and cooperative atmosphere. And yet this is for a relatively standardized type of product!

Theoretical implications

The most important implication of the existence of relationships is that companies cannot be regarded as independent units that can chose counterparts at any time, but rather as units interlocked with each other, constituting highly specialized and complex structures. Earlier, the border of the company was seen as the dividing line between cooperation and conflict - cooperation within the company and conflict in relation to all external units. The corresponding means for coordination are hierarchy and the market mechanism[3]. The existence of relationships makes this picture much more diffuse. There are great opportunities for cooperation with a lot of external units forming, for example, coalitions. Thus, it is often more fruitful to see the company as a part of a network instead of a free and independent actor in an atomistic market.

A Network Approach

Relationships connect companies into structures that preferably can be analysed using network concepts[4]. The characteristics of a network are described by Cook & Emerson (1978, p. 725) as *sets of two or more connected exchange relations*. The connection can be positive (if exchange in one is contingent upon exchange in the other) or negative (if exchange in one is contingent upon nonexchange in the other), they can be in the form of relationships or as more general dependencies (*ibid.* p. 725). There are, as one example, technical dependencies between companies that either use the same technology, deliver to customers with a certain technology or buy from suppliers using the same technology. In these three cases it is also easy to find both positive and negative connections.

Against this background a network approach seems to be a promising tool when analysing technical development. In this section such a framework will be presented and illustrated.

This network model has been developed by Håkansson & Johanson (1984) based on earlier works such as Hammarkvist, Håkansson and Mattsson (1982), Hägg & Johanson (eds., 1982), Håkansson (1982), and Mattsson (1985). There, basic classes of variables related respectively to the actors, the activities and the resources are identified.

These variables are related to each other in a general structure of a network. This implies that at the same time there exist both conflicting and cooperative elements between different actors, different activities and different resources. (ibid. p. 1)

The variables are defined in relation to each other which can be seen in the following description of each of them.

Actors

Those who perform activities and/or control resources within a certain field are defined as actors. It can be individuals, a group of persons, a division within a company, a company, or a group of companies constituting a coalition. Thus, in a network there are often actors at different organizational levels and furthermore an actor at one level can be part of an actor at a higher level[5].

Each actor can be described in three dimensions:

–which activities the actor performs or controls
–which resources the actor controls

14

–the knowledge the actor has about activities, resources and other actors in the network.

The actor's main aim is supposed to be to increase its control in the network. In that struggle the actors are using their experience and knowledge of the network as well as their relationships with others in order to improve their position. They are 'networking'. Potentially there is a large number of different actors that can be involved in a technical development project together with a focal company. They can be suppliers of equipment, components, materials, etc; customers or customers' customers, trade research institutes or departments at universities, consultants or producers of complementary products, and competitors. Each of these potential cooperating partners has certain resources including some special knowledge of resources, activities or other actors.

Activities

Activities are performed by the actors which means that resources are combined, developed, exchanged or created by use of other resources. Two main categories of activities can be identified: transformation and transaction activities. Transformation activities are always carried out within the control of one actor, and are characterized by one resource being improved by the use of other resources. Transaction activities link transformation activities, forming chains of activities, and creating relationships with other actors. Activities are linked to each other in various ways. They constitute parts of more or less repetitive activity cycles, where a number of interdependent activities are repeated. In order to make an activity cycle complete, both transformation and transaction activities are needed. The duration or extent of a transformation activity is always arbitrary. Thus, one specific transformation activity can be divided into smaller ones separated by transactions or extended by integrating earlier or later transformation activities and thereby excluding transactions.

In a given network, series of activities forming repetitive activity cycles can be identified. Some of these cycles are tightly connected with each other, forming transaction chains while others are much more loosely connected.

There is a strong interdependence between actors and activi-

15

ties as the former learn to perform the activities in such a way that activity cycles and transaction chains become more efficient. This experience creates routines and informal rules which bring about stability through repetivity.

The network of linked activities is normally characterized by redundancy insofar as certain single activities can often be taken away without destroying the network. The network remains and functions, although not so effectively, when an activity is taken away because associated activities are adjusted a little in order to take over the function of the absent activity. Furthermore the network is always imperfect in the sense that changes in the activities (new ones, rearrangements, etc.) can make it more efficient[6].

The focus in this book is on transaction activities. Especially transaction activities including various types of technical cooperation. But, as indicated above transaction activities are directly connected to transformation activities and thereby influenced by their characteristics.

Resources

Resources consist of physical assets (machinery, material, etc), financial assets, and human assets (labour, knowledge and relationships). Transformation resources and transaction resources are mutually dependent. The use of and the value of a specific transformation resource is always dependent on how it is combined with transaction resources and vice versa. If the same resource is used in another activity cycle other dimensions of it can be utilized and the value of it can be different.

Knowledge and experience of resources are important. By combining resources new knowledge can emerge which gives possibilities for new and improved combinations. New insights in the handling of resources can change or break old activity cycles and therefore contain the seeds of development and change in the network.

In the following chapters a lot of examples will be given of how different actors combine their resources in development projects; the combination of knowledge about the use of a process with production knowledge of the supplier, the new product of the supplier that is tested out within the production process of the customer, the general knowledge about a certain production

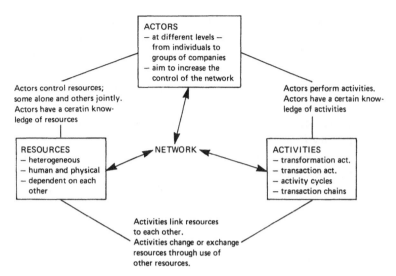

Figure 1:1 Network Model.

process that is combined with the general knowledge of another production process, and so on. The only limitation on the possible number of combinations of resources is that of human creativity.

Network

The elements within each of the three basic classes of variables form within them a network structure. Each actor is related to other actors, some in a positive way, others in a negative way and together they form a network[7]. The same is true for the activities and the resources. Furthermore these three networks are closely connected with each other. They are intervowen in a total network (see Figure 1:1). There are some specific forces that bind the three networks together. These are according to Håkansson & Johanson (1984, p. 9):

1. Functional interdependence: Actors, activities and resources together form a system in which heterogeneous demands are combined with heterogeneous supply. They are thus functionally related to each other.

2. Power structure; The actors base their power on the control of activities and/or resources. Thus, there is a system-

17

atic handling of the different components in relation to each other - they are organized by conscious hands.

3. Knowledge structure; The design of the activities as well as the use of the resources are bound together by the knowledge and the experience of previous and earlier actors.

4. Time related structure; The network is a product of its history in terms of experience and investments in relationships, knowledge, routines and so on. Changes of the network must be accepted by the rest of the network (or at least by some part of it). Therefore most of the changes will be marginal and closely related to the past.

All four forces point to the close and maybe unexpected connection between stability and development. Development in certain dimensions needs stability in others or can be a means to preserve stability in others. Development in, for example, the activities can be a means to secure stability in regard to the power structure. Stability in terms of a close relationship can be important when one actor tries to develop a new way to use some resources. A development project together with a customer can be one way to stabilize the relationship with him. This duality between stability and development will be one of the themes in the following chapters which mainly concern technical development within different kinds of networks.

An illustration of the network model

Before describing the content of the book an empirical illustration to the network model will be given. Let us start with the use of a product - large engines for marine applications. There are few companies specialized in producing large engines and who compete world-wide. The users are the ship-owners but the buying company can be the shipyard with quite different interests. The use of the engine from an economical point of view is very much dependent on the kind of fuel used. If cheaper oil (for example heavy oil) can be used this decreases the costs. Thus, there is a technical and economic connection to the oil companies. Furthermore in order to use heavy oil products, special equipment - a separator - is needed. This product is manufactured by a few producers who also market their products world-wide.

18

All these different companies are basically involved in different transaction chains and they are very much affected by the type of transformation and transaction activities that they perform in combination with the resources they need to control. The oil companies are process industries which need to control the raw material. The engine and separator producers are mechanical engineering companies where the most important resource is probably the market which can be controlled by a large marketing and service organization. The ship-owners are service producing companies, and so on. All these companies are, however, also connected through the fact that they can all influence the use of large marine engines. This connection also means that their resources to some degree are related and dependent on each other. In a special cooperation project (described in Chapter 3) where the aim was to develop the use of cheap fuel one large producer within the separator group (Alfa-Laval) cooperated with the largest engine producer (Sulzer) and one of the largest oil companies (SHELL).

Managerial Issues

Important managerial issues related to the innovation process will be discussed in relation to six different managerial positions. The first five are related to activities within the individual company whilst the sixth relates to wider issues with implications for policies and actions at the whole industry, regional, and/or national level.

On the company level we will start with the project manager.

Project Manager

For a manager responsible for a certain development project the following cooperation issues can be identified:

• to identify potential external cooperation partners: these can be units that the company already has relationships with or new ones.
• to establish a dialogue on technical matters related to the project with the most promising partners.

19

• to find suitable cooperation forms with those partners where cooperation is established.

• to manage the cooperation project: to give support and create an atmosphere of optimism for the members of the project and to revise and change it in relation to its development.

• to finalize and end the project in an appropriate way.

All the above issues must be handled in a way that is adapted to the characteristics of the project. But the way of acting ought also to be a part of the company's strategy in cooperation matters.

R&D Managers

The R&D manager has among other things the responsibility for the company's total development activities which includes the above mentioned issue regarding its cooperation strategy. More detailed issues relevant to the R&D manager are:

• in order to effectively use external counterparts in the company's technical development several company functions have to be involved. This increases the need for a 'technical development center' where all threads are bound together. This is a task for the R&D manager.

• a related task is to handle the interface between different departments such as marketing, purchasing, production and R&D.

• the management should promote a technology policy including the use of external units. This should, however, always be adjusted to changes (internal as well as external). This managment policy must be a living and never ending readjustment process.

• to combine different projects into some kind of logical whole, which, however, could and even should include different kinds of contradictions.

• to market the company's 'needs' and 'abilities' toward different types of counterparts.

• to identify, handle, and react to potential cooperation partners which includes finding appropriate cooperation forms.

• to identify and react to actual or potential competitors (companies or groups of companies) in regard to technical development.

Purchasing Manager

The purchasing manager is responsible for the interface between the company and its suppliers. Several of these are usually important to the company's technical development and therefore potential cooperation partners. The purchasing manager, thus, must be highly involved in the following issues:

• to continually follow up supplier markets and individual suppliers from a technical point of view.
• to develop relationships with potential cooperation partners as well as taking care of the chances that occur in the already established supplier relationships.
• to handle cooperation and conflict in the relationships - sometimes there is the need to increase the conflict elements in order to vitalize the relationships and in other situations the cooperative elements must be underlined in order to get things done.

Marketing Manager

The marketing manager has a very similiar position to the purchasing manager - the only difference is that the counterparts are customers instead of suppliers. Some major issues are:

• to identify and to follow up the development of the customers' needs from a technical point of view by watching their investments, new products and so on.
• to find suitable cooperation partners, which for example might be customers with highly demanding requirements. These can be unprofitable and also awkward as they are demanding, but this can in the long run sharpen the company's performance which can give positive effects in relation to other less demanding customers.
• to watch the cooperation between competing producers and their customers as well as the development of substitutes.

General Manager

The questions raised in this book are directly related to the development of the whole company and in this way of utmost importance to general managers. All the issues identified with the four other positions are in different ways also relevant to the general manager. We will not repeat these issues again. Instead the tasks of the general manager from this point of view can be summarized as follows:

• to balance internal and external development work against each other. In order to be an attractive counterpart in technical development cooperation the company has to have a certain minimum of internal development resources that are considered valuable by potential counterparts. The 'right' balance between the use of internal and external resources, however, can be quite different from company to company due to varying internal as well as external factors.

• to establish the company's position within the technical network, which includes establishing cooperative relationships as well as mapping out important counterparts and their relationships. The position must furthermore be defended and altered in response to different changes.

Industrial Policy Makers

The questions discussed previously are of importance to politicians and governmental units dealing with aggregates of companies since important policy issues can be identified which relate to the function of an industry, a geographical region or a whole nation from a technological development point of view. Interest in these types of policies has increased substantially among politicians during the last ten years due to the rapid structural changes in many mature industries and accompanying regional crises. The success of, for example, Japanese companies has also increased the interest in these questions. One underlying factor for their success is believed to be policies of the Japanese government. Concepts such as industry targeting have developed. Several relevant issues can be identified by using our frame of reference. The most important ones are:

22

• to identify relevant networks of companies. In many situations the grouping of companies into industries is not applicable as important relationships often cross industrial boundaries. For example, in a project concerning the technical development within the 'wood-saw-network', companies belonging to the steel, engineering, electronic, data software and the saw mill industries were identified as important actors.

• to create and encourage exchange between different technical areas. This can be in the form of technical meetings, temporarily as conferences, more permanently as science parks, or through joint projects between companies from different industries. The aim is to enrich and fertilize the network structure, include new companies, develop relationships, etc.

• to balance and handle power structure: developments within a certain field can easily be blocked or at least delayed if strong interests are mobilized against the development or mobilized in favour of radically alternative development paths.

The last point indicates the importance of being able to interpret and handle power structures. If the power structure is not understood and handled in the right way, a good idea or product can be ignored as is illustrated by the following example.

A trade research institute in Sweden succeeded in solving a technical problem put forward by several companies within one industry. The solution meant that a new product opportunity was identified. This opportunity was passed on to several competing companies in a democratic way. One year later when nothing had emerged the researcher responsible for the project asked one of the companies why they did not launch the product. The answer was that the company did not find it worthwile to make the necessary market investments (to teach the customers how to use the product), since they knew that when this had been done the competitors could launch the same product. As the manager said:'technical knowledge known by everybody is not a good base for business'.

The lesson is that the use of knowledge also has a political-power aspect which is directly related to the existing structure. This must always be considered when evaluating different activities.

Content of the Book

Chapter 2 focuses on process development and describes and analyses how production processes have been developed and brought into use by cooperation between different companies. The focus is very much on the interaction between the companies within these development projects and the development process is furthermore mainly seen from the process user's point of view. The chapter contains recommendations as to how such projects should be organized and handled in order to be successful.

In Chapter 3 a more global network approach is used to analyse product development as part of total technical development. Again interesting issues and implications for management emerge in this chapter.

Technical cooperation as a part of the procurement strategy is analysed in Chapter 4. In order to develop their competitive strength manufacturing companies can use their suppliers in different ways and usually in a much more extensive way than today. The strategy is, however, dependent both on the purchasing company's characteristics and on the characteristics of the network.

The network - both actors and relationships - consists of individuals. Among the individuals we have special professional groups. These groups have similar backgrounds in some way - for example the same education. Furthermore they often have special clubs or meetings or other 'group' identities. In Chapter 5 the contact network of such a group of professionals, metallurgical engineers, which as a group has been called the mafia of the Swedish steel industry, is analysed. To the individual company this type of analysis is important, for example, when recruiting a new manager.

Finally, in the last chapter, general strategic implications for industrial companies are examined in terms of how to understand and effectively manage technical cooperation and development within networks.

Notes to Chapter 1

1. Another important explanation factor of this way of approaching technical development at the company level is neoclassical economic theory. The interest is there focused on the individual actor - the firm - and its behaviour in relation to input and output markets.

2. This type of recommendation is very common in marketing management text books. From a theoretical point of view they are based on the marketing mix approach which in turn is heavily influenced by neoclassical economic theory.

3. See Williamson (1975) and (1979) for a more extensive discussion of these two types of coordination mechanisms.

4. For overviews see Aldrich & Whetten (1981), Aldrich (1979) and Rogers & Kincaid (1981).

5. The concept 'main actors' is used in order to identify the principal actors within the network.

6. Such imperfections of the network are extremely important from a theoretical point of view as they clearly distinguish the network concept from the market concept. A network relates resources of different kinds to each other and there will always be possibilities to improve the use of at least some of these by changing activities or by adding new types of resources. It is, therefore, meaningless to try to estimate the optimality of a network per se. It can only be evaluated from the standpoint of individuals or groups of actors.

7. One problem is to limit the network. Epstein (1969) has suggested the concept 'effective network' to describe those who *interact most intensely and most regularly, and who are therefore likely to come to know each other* and to let the remainder form the *extended network* (pp. 110-11).

Chapter Two

PROCESS INNOVATION THROUGH TECHNICAL COOPERATION

Jens Laage-Hellman

Process Innovation

In this chapter we shall describe how new process technology can be developed through cooperation between different units in the network. We argue that for individual firms the effectiveness of the process development efforts can often be increased by interaction with external units such as equipment suppliers, research institutes or companies competing in the same industry. The reason is that these other units have valuable resources and skills which can be made available through various cooperative ventures. Before developing this argument, however, we shall first comment on the concept of process innovation and the importance of process development in different types of industries and companies.

In the literature a distinction is commonly made between product and process innovations (see e.g. Utterback & Abernathy, 1975). The former are concerned with new technologies or combinations of technologies introduced commercially to meet user or market needs. Process innovations on the other hand are concerned with the equipment, methods and systems employed to produce the products. In practice, however, it is often very difficult to distinguish between process and product development. Firstly, process and product innovations are frequently combined in the sense that new process technology is used to make new products. Secondly, what is thought of as a process innovation by one firm, e.g. a semiconductor company, may be considered by another, e.g. a machinery supplier, as a product innovation. In this chapter we shall use the term process innovation as seen from the perspective of the process users. Thus, we shall talk about process innovations whether the technical development activities are performed by the users themselves or by outside suppliers.

Different types of process innovations

A company may engage in process development for a variety of reasons. The purpose can be to reduce production costs by improving output productivity or material yields, increasing scale, reducing energy consumption or using cheaper raw materials. Alternatively the objective may be to improve product quality or make it possible to produce products with new features. The Pilkington float glass process and the continuous casting of steel are two well-known examples of process innovations which have led to substantial cost savings in the production of existing products. The planar process used in the manufacture of integrated circuits can be mentioned as an example of a process advancement which made it possible to introduce revolutionary new products onto the market.

The above-mentioned process innovations are examples of leap-wise progress in production technology. Such innovations are relatively rare, but when they occur they often have a long-term, far-reaching effect on competition[1]. The bulk of process development is of an evolutionary rather than a revolutionary nature. By minor incremental changes a given production process typically develops toward increasingly higher levels of performance. For example, since the invention of the planar process in 1959 the number of elements that can be put on a single chip has increased constantly at a high rate. Until the mid 1970s this development toward constantly smaller and more complex integrated circuits was rendered possible by the continuous improvements made in process technology. Thus, the limit to product complexity was the ability to fabricate the chips. During the last decade the situation has changed. Today the main limiting factor is the difficulty of designing rather than of processing (Penfield Jr, 1982).

Even though each individual improvement is marginal the current 'everyday rationalizations' in operations lead to substantial effects over time. This is illustrated by the following example which is based on a Swedish study of technical development and industry structure. The example concerns a hot rolling mill for steel strips which was installed in 1952. During the following 25 years no technical changes were made except for the replacement of worn parts. Despite this the productivity (man-hours per kg) increased each year by 3.7% on average. It has thus been possible to double the capacity in 17-18 years without investing in new equipment. The most important factors behind this evolution proved to be continual changes in product mix, increasing degree of product standardization and increasing slab weight. As this example clearly shows the cost-efficiency in a plant can thus be dramatically improved without introducing new technology. In other words the efficiency is not only a function of which technology is used, but also to a large extent of how it is used and developed (Carlsson *et al.*, 1979).

We have seen above that process innovations can be characterized in two dimensions, viz. the degree of radicalness, and whether the main benefit is cost reduction or improved product performance. By combining these two dimensions we can form a four-field matrix containing four main categories of process innovation (see Figure 2:1). It is reasonable to assume that the pattern of external cooperation differs among these four categories, e.g. with regard to the type of partner.

Thus, process development activities aimed at reducing the cost level in the existing plant tend to take place jointly with the existing suppliers of equipment, raw materials and operating supplies. When the main objective of the process development activities is to improve the product performance it is natural to interact also with the current users of the products. When it comes to more significant process innovations we can hypothesize that the suppliers of key equipment and research institutions of different kinds are two important types of cooperation partner. In the case of major process innovations leading to lower production costs for existing products, other firms competing in the same industry may also constitute potential partners. By establishing a joint venture with such companies the R&D costs for developing a new process can sometimes be substantially reduced. However, if the purpose of the process innovation is to enable the company to produce new types of product, cooperation with competitors is probably not conceivable for obvious reasons.

In this chapter we shall deal primarily with major advancements in process technology. This does not mean that we neglect

Main benefit

		Cost reduction	Product performance
Degree of radicalness	Minor incremental improvement	Suppliers of equipment, raw materials and operating supplies	Suppliers of equipment, raw materials and operating supplies. Product users
	Major advancement	Key equipment suppliers Research institutions Other firms competing in the same industry	Key equipment suppliers Research institutions

Figure 2:1 Four main Categories of Process Innovation. The most Common Types of Cooperation Partner are Mentioned for each Category.

the importance of technical exchange in incremental innovation. On the contrary we already know from earlier studies that technical contacts within established supplier-customer relationships are very common and play a crucial role for the everyday improvements of existing products and production processes (see e.g. Håkansson, ed., 1982). Instead we have chosen to put our argument to the test by focusing on the other extreme, i.e. the development of radically new processes. In these situations the role of relationships is perhaps not equally obvious. Received theory often emphasizes the role of the individual innovator. Major technological innovations are frequently associated with one person or one firm who has made the basic invention or scientific discovery (e.g. Pilkington - the float glass process, Xerox - the copying machine, Bell Laboratories/Shockley - the transistor, etc). Technical cooperation within inter-organizational relationships is seldom mentioned as a critical factor behind major innovations. We would like to question this picture which we think is too one-sided and simplified. If we can point to the significance of cooperation this would indicate that the current picture of the innovation process has to be somewhat revised. The inclusion of R&D cooperation as an important component in the theory of innovation would have major implications both for business managers and policy makers.

The importance of process innovation as a competitive means

Process development is pursued by companies in all types of industries and networks. It is reasonable to believe, however, that process innovation as a competitive means is particularly important in capital-intensive industries such as the chemical, pulp and paper, and steel industries. Especially for firms pursuing a cost leadership strategy, the introduction of improved process technology can be an effective way of gaining competitive advantages over rivals (see e.g. Porter, 1983). In fields where the product characteristics are strongly dependent on the production methods process innovation can also be used as a means to achieve market leadership through product differentiation. For example, firms engaged in the production of alloyed steels, specialty chemicals or pharmaceuticals frequently seek to attain competitiveness based on an ability to produce products with superior properties or a unique set of characteristics.

It should be noticed that the production technology is important for the competitiveness not only in the process industries. As a result of the technological development the capital-intensity is increasing in many other industries. A rapid development in manufacturing technology is at present in progress in the electronics and mechanical engineering industries. Large resources are invested especially in the field of computer-aided engineering (CAE). The introduction of new techniques such as CAD, CAM and FMS makes it possible to produce existing products at less cost, with greater accuracy and in a shorter time. The number of large-scale CAE systems now in operation is still relatively small. However, these new production techniques are judged to have great potential and a growing number of firms are identifying the substantial competitive advantages offered by computer aided engineering (Blois, 1984). Above all the FMS offers significant benefits to companies which produce items in medium and large batch sizes where there are frequent changes in manufacturing requirements (Parkinson & Avlonitis, 1984).

The importance of process innovation does not only vary across different industries. According to the life cycle model there is also a development over time within each industry (see e.g. Utterback & Abernathy, 1975). Thus, the mode of technological change is thought to vary as a product or industry moves through the life cycle. During the early stages technological emphasis is focused on product innovation, and process development in general is of minor significance. Later, as the industry matures process innovation toward lower costs takes over as the dominant form of technological activity. Then as the industry develops toward increasingly higher degrees of capital-intensity and product standardization major process innovation also diminishes and the focus shifts to cumulative improvements of existing processes.

According to this pattern the rate of process innovation is highest in the middle of the life cycle. The strategic importance of new process development is therefore especially great for firms in this stage of development. From this it follows that revolutionary change in process technology tends to be instituted by established firms in the industry (in contrast to major product innovations which are more often introduced by new entrants). Examples are the Pilkington float glass process, Mobil's zeolite catalyst and ICI's pruteen plant - all revolutionary process innovations (Utterback, 1982).

Process Technology Networks

As suggested in the previous chapter technological development in industrial markets can be characterized as an interplay between different organizations where interdependent activities are taking place simultaneously in different parts of the network. Certain development activities are carried out within individual units, others are pursued in cooperation between two or more units.

Members of the network

In general there are three main categories of unit which are involved in the development of a certain process technology (such as steel melting, petroleum refining or automobile assembly). These are the process users (e.g. steelworks, oil companies or automobile manufacturers), the equipment suppliers to these firms, and independent research organizations doing research work in relevant fields (e.g. universities and trade research institutes). Together these units make up a process technology network. The members of such a network contribute to the development of the technology either by working alone or through cooperating with other units. Cooperative R&D may take place between firms in the same category (e.g. two process users) or between different types of firm (e.g. a process user and a supplier).

Different types of unit in the network typically play different roles in the innovation process. According to a common idea the main role of the research organizations is to produce basic knowledge. This knowledge is then used by manufacturing firms in developing equipment and processes which are subsequently sold to the end-users. However, the distribution of roles is much more complex and less differentiated than suggested by this model. First of all, the role of the research organizations is not only to produce new knowledge but, perhaps to an even larger extent, to transmit existing knowledge within the network. Certain research institutes may also engage in applied research aiming at the development of new processes and industrial uses. Futhermore, there is no clear-cut division of roles between the suppliers and the users. Process innovations may have their origins with either type of unit.

We can conceive of different types of network exhibiting different features with regard to the locus of process innovation. Certain technology networks can thus be characterized as 'research dominated', i.e. the development of process technology takes place primarily at universities or research institutes. Other networks can be said to be 'user dominated' or 'supplier dominated'[2]. In the former it is the users who dominate the process development while in the latter new processes are to a larger extent developed by equipment manufacturers or engineering firms. We shall try to illustrate this reasoning by giving some empirical examples.

Research dominated networks

'The Swedish laser processing network' can be taken as an example of a research dominated network. The following discussion is based on a study that we carried out in 1982 (Håkansson *et al.*, 1983). It was performed on behalf of STU (the National Board for Technical Development) and focused on the industry - researcher interaction within six research programs financed by STU. One of these dealt with laser processing and laser production equipment[3].

In Figure 2:2 we have tried to illustrate this network as it appeared at the time when the study was made. We do not have enough data for a complete description covering all units and relationships (nor was this the purpose of the study). However, we believe that we have captured at least the principal features of the network.

As we shall see below a key position in the network is held by three research institutions at the Technical University of Luleå, Chalmers University of Technology and the National Defence Research Institute (FOA) respectively. Other important members were the 10-15 engineering firms with their own laser processing equipment or current development programs in the field. Some of them are mentioned in the figure. In addition there were hundreds of other firms which had contracted out laser processing, or carried out application tests with other firms or with the research institutions. Radians Innova was a spin-off company linked to Chalmers. It was created in order to facilitate the commercial exploitation of the competence built up at the institution. (Later a similar company, Prelucor, was formed by the laser researchers in Luleå.)

There were no Swedish laser manufacturing companies but some of the foreign suppliers were represented in Sweden by independent agents or laser processing firms.

Laser processing can be divided into two main application fields. One is macroprocessing with high power lasers, such as cutting and drilling, heat treatment and welding. The other is microprocessing with low power lasers. Typical applications are drilling of small holes and trimming of integrated circuits. Luleå

33

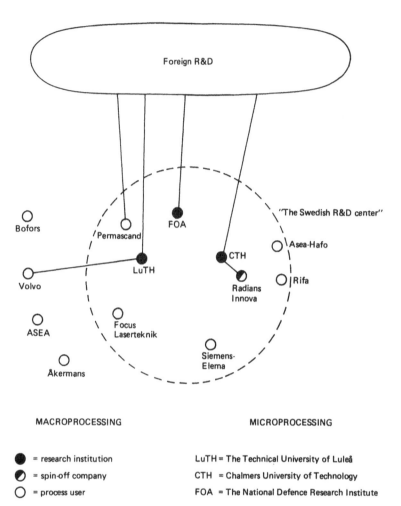

Figure 2:2 The Swedish Laser Processing Network.

had specialized in the former field while Chalmers had equipment and knowledge primarily suited for microprocessing. FOA had a medium-sized laser.

As indicated in Figure 2:2 it is possible to identify something which can be called a Swedish 'R&D center'. It consisted of those units which had great knowledge/experience of laser processing or possessed their own R&D facilities. At that time the three research institutions played a central role in the network. Together they represented the main part of the laser processing

R&D in Sweden. Since 1980 they had participated in a large research program started and financed by STU. The background was that the level of laser use had been considered too low in Sweden. In several other countries, especially the USA, Japan, West Germany and Great Britain, lasers had already made a breakthrough as a process tool. The goal of the STU program was therefore to establish a knowledge base and expertise in the field and transfer these to the industry. To increase the relevance of the research work and facilitate the spread of knowledge, representatives of four engineering firms were invited to join the steering group for the program. Focus Laserteknik and Siemens-Elema were both selected because they already had experience of industrial laser processing. Volvo and ASEA were chosen as they were large, technically advanced companies which had shown interest in adopting the laser processing technology.

An important user who was not represented in the steering group was Permascand. This company was owned jointly by Kema Nobel and an American firm. Permascand was a pioneer and had invested large resources in laser processing. They had two lasers which were used for their own production, contract manufacture and R&D assignments (testing of different applications for potential laser users). Permascand was also an agent for two US laser manufacturers. Through internal R&D activities, external assignments and, not least, the contacts with sister companies in the American group Permascand had been able to build up a large competence in the field, and considered themselves to be the leading company in Sweden. They had some contacts with the two academic institutions but had not made use of the research results as they had already acquired this knowledge.

Other experienced users who were not involved in the STU program are Rifa (the Ericsson Group) and Asea-Hafo, the two major producers of electronic components in Sweden. Both have used lasers since the early 1970s. Rifa was one of the first component manufacturers in Europe to adopt the laser processing technology. This had required a great deal of development work which had been carried out within the company. Apart from the continuous contacts with the American equipment manufacturers Rifa had had no technical contacts at all regarding the laser technology with external units in Sweden or abroad.

Obviously the role of the Swedish research units in this network was to acquire and transmit to Swedish end-users a knowledge which to a large extent already existed abroad. As a consequence the monitoring of foreign R&D and the build-up of contacts with foreign experts have been important tasks for the researchers. Furthermore, the research teams, especially those at the two universities, have been very active in advocating the industrial use of lasers in Sweden They have accomplished this mission not only by spreading information through research reports, articles, seminars and courses. More importantly they have established direct relationships with potential users. As a service to the industry they have offered to make tests on practical applications at the request of individual clients. This important, greatly appreciated assignment business has now in large measure been taken over by the two spin-off companies.

As an example of a closer development relationship within the network we can mention that Volvo has developed an extensive technical cooperation with the research team at Luleå. On a contract basis the laser researchers have explored several applications of great interest to Volvo. Volvo has even bought a laser which has been placed in Luleå to be used in the joint studies. Among other things there was a need to develop auxiliary equipment and control systems. Together with the Volvo people the researchers have also travelled around and visited different laser suppliers.

The dominant role of the research institutions in this network was a result of the generally low technological level of the Swedish end-users and the task given to them by STU. If there had been a major manufacturer of laser processing equipment in Sweden the picture would probably have been somewhat different. Then it would have been easier for the would-be users to obtain technical assistance from the supplier side. Now, when most equipment suppliers were located in the United States it was only feasible for big companies to establish supplier relationships with a high technical content. For most potential users starting to build up their own competence in the field the research institutions and their associated spin-off companies constituted a valuable source of technology. Permascand, being an agent and having technical service facilities at the same time, can to some extent be said to have played the role of a domestic equipment manufacturer. They had carried out some 50 major development assignments. In total they had had contacts with more than 300 Swedish firms.

User and supplier dominated networks

To exemplify user dominated process development we can refer to the work of von Hippel (1977). In a study conducted in the United States he found that 67% of the new process machines employed in the manufacture of semiconductors and electronic subassemblies were developed by the users, not by the machinery manufacturers. This network can thus be characterized as user dominated. In contrast a supplier dominated pattern seems to prevail in the chemical field (see Baranson, 1978, Ch.6). Here new processes more often originate from chemical engineering firms specializing in the development and sale of process technology. These firms are seldom end-users of the processes they develop. Their business is to commercialize R&D results into processes and engineering services from technologically based proprietary positions in various product fields. The chemical engineering firms often do much of the original process development work themselves but may also collaborate closely with chemical firms who develop their own processes. Then, acting partially as agents for the process developer, the engineering firms may adapt the process to their clients' requirements.

There may not only be a division of roles between the different types of unit. Within each category different firms typically play different roles in the innovation process. Some firms strive for technological leadership in process technology while others perform the role of technological followers. Because of the high costs often inherent in the development of new processes the technological leadership strategy is in many fields only feasible for large companies[4].

User-supplier cooperation within the network

As already mentioned we focus in this book on the interaction between different units in the network. By cooperating in various ways companies can sometimes develop new or improved technologies more effectively than would otherwise be the case. The reason is that different units have different resources and skills which are complementary in nature. For example, the suppliers of process equipment are specialists in designing, engineering and manufacturing the hardware while the process users have the application knowledge and production experience. It is therefore not surprising that new process technology is often the result of cooperative R&D ventures between equipment suppliers or engineering firms on the one hand and end-users on the other. By combining their respective skills and resources synergistic effects can be created in the development work. Later in this chapter we shall describe in detail two cases from 'the special steelmaking network'. As an example of user-supplier interaction in the pulpmaking field we can mention here the development of the CTMP process (CTMP= chemical thermo-mechanical pulp). This technology, which can be characterized as a major breakthrough in pulping, was to a large extent developed in cooperation between an equipment manufacturer (Sunds Defibrator) and SCA, which is one of the major pulp and paper companies in Sweden. Sunds Defibrator happens to be a subsidiary of SCA which probably facilitated the cooperation. Nonetheless the CTMP process is a good example of what can be achieved when a process user and a machinery supplier coordinate their development efforts. The CTMP process was subsequently commercialized by Sunds Defibrator which at present holds a two-third share of the world market for this technology.

The recent construction of a highly automated assembly factory for automobile engines can be taken as an example of a successful user-supplier interaction in mechanical engineering. This is Saab-Scania which has invested large resources in new manufacturing technology in its Södertälje plant. It has become one of the most advanced engine factories in the world. Many of the assembly operations have been automated by means of industrial robots and automatic material handling systems. The new factory is considered to be a real breakthrough for automated assembly, a field which up to now has been difficult to robotize.

The technology has been developed together with ASEA and several other Swedish equipment suppliers. ASEA, which is Europe's leading manufacturer of industrial robots, has shared the development responsibility with Saab-Scania. For ASEA this joint development venture opens up a new marketing opportunity. ASEA can now go out and sell the new assembly technology to other automobile manufacturers. The Södertälje plant will then serve as a valuable reference. This is accepted by Saab-Scania which is only too willing to demonstrate its plant to its competitors. There is a gentlemens' agreement among automobile companies to share production technology. One of the responsible engineers at Saab-Scania says: *We learn from each other. We are not afraid of industrial espionage. Our factory is custom-made, and those who believe that one can copy a factory make a mistake.* Saab-Scania does not have the resources nor the interest to commercialize the assembly technology itself. Instead it will be ASEA which will try to make money on the new technology. ASEA has already sold numerous robots to automobile manufacturers throughout the world. However, so far very few of these are used for assembly operations. (Ny Teknik, 1983)

Process Development Interaction from the Perspective of the Process User

Different approaches to process development cooperation

Let us now look at process development interaction from the perspective of the individual firm. Basically the process user has the choice of developing the process technology it needs within the company or relying to a greater or lesser extent on external sources of technology. Figure 2:3 shows how the innovation process can be characterized along a scale representing varying degrees of external involvement. At one extreme all process development activities are carried out internally. It may for example be a semiconductor company inventing, designing and building a machine to be used in its own production plant. At the other extreme the company acquires process technology which has been developed by others (e.g. machine builders, engineering firms, research institutes or other process users). The purchasing of turn-key plants falls into this category.

Between these two extremes we have different degrees and forms of development interaction. Process development cooperation means that both parties play an active part in a certain project and aim at a common goal (such as developing a completely new process, designing a new piece of equipment, or solving a certain production problem).

39

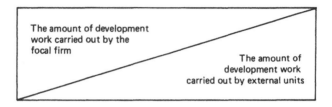

Figure 2:3 Scale Representing the Relative Activity of a Focal Firm and External Units in Process Development.

In practice it is difficult to find cases representing the extreme ends of the scale. In general the real extreme cases lie on the scale slightly inward from the ends. Thus, a firm pursuing an internally oriented process development strategy normally interacts with a few or many external units in order to obtain ideas or information as an input to its own R&D activities. It may also need to engage consultants to solve certain technical problems or use external laboratories or pilot-plant facilities. In the case of technology acquisition the technology to be transferred often has to be somewhat adapted to the buyer's specific needs and wants. As a result the development work cannot be completely left to the technology supplier. Normally the focal firm will have to carry out certain R&D activities itself, either internally or together with the supplier (e.g. joint testing of different technical solutions). Under all circumstances a more or less intensive information exchange will be necessary to make the required adaptation or further development possible. Needless to say the technology transfer itself usually implies many technical contacts between the two firms.

The different positions on the scale in Figure 2:3 correspond to different approaches to process development cooperation which can be used by a firm (or an individual division, business unit, production plant or project group). The choice of a cooperative approach is of strategic importance as it influences both the outcome of the process development efforts and the requirements for the firm's own technical resources and organization. Given certain internal and external conditions an 'introvert strategy' is sometimes the most suitable. As we have already pointed out, however, the use of external units as information sources, cooperation partners or technology suppliers offers great potential advantages in many situations[5].

The laser processing network presents some examples of different cooperative approaches. Permascand, for instance, built up a high competence without cooperating with 'the Swedish R&D center'. This approach can partly be explained by the fact that Permascand was a pioneer in Sweden. At the time when Permascand entered the field the Swedish laser research was still rather marginal, so they could obtain little help from that side. Instead they chose to establish relationships with foreign suppliers and users, primarily in the United States. They have also learnt a great deal through their own internal R&D and by carrying out tests and contract processing for a large number of Swedish firms. Later on when Volvo decided to enter the field the STU research program was under way. Through its membership in the steering group Volvo gained insight into the program and an opportunity to establish contacts with the research teams. As we have already said this led to the start of a joint development project with the Technical University of Luleå. Volvo thus chose to build up its know-how and develop applications through collaboration with an external unit. In this case the unit was an academic research institution. One reason was that Volvo wanted to cooperate with a body which stood aloof from commercial interests. This excluded Permascand and other firms representing laser equipment manufacturers. At an earlier stage Volvo had considered entering into cooperation with Fiat. Fiat has its own laser laboratory and is considered to be one of the leading laser users in Europe. This cooperation was not realized as Volvo at that time did not feel ready for such a big project. Bofors is another company which has been developing different laser processing applications. In contrast to Volvo, Bofors has not tried to use the domestic research resources. Instead they have relied on foreign equipment suppliers which have given them all the technical assistance they needed.

Some management problems

One general conclusion that we can draw from our study of the Swedish research programs is that knowledge about the network is essential for effective use of the external resources. The company needs to know where to find different types of resource, the roles played by different units, how to use particular resources, etc. This type of knowledge can only be acquired by taking an active part in the technical development of the network and by interacting with other units. This is what we can call 'networking'. It gives a feeling for what is going on within the network. Without such a feeling or knowledge it is difficult to evaluate information, to identify cooperative opportunities and to know how to act in different situations (e.g. when another company comes with a proposal to cooperate). It takes time to build up this network-specific knowledge. One implication is therefore that companies need to have a long-term approach if they want to pursue an 'extrovert R&D strategy'. The creation of interactive channels should be regarded as investments which will yield a positive return only in the long run.

We have here emphasized the advantages of using external development resources. It should not be disregarded, however, that such an approach is also associated with certain difficulties and risks. To be able to take advantage of the potential benefits the firm has to find suitable and cooperative counterparts and learn how to handle the technical exchange with these.

Let us point out some dangers and risks which a process user or supplier can meet when trying to develop cooperation with external units.

Firstly, the firm may have trouble in interesting these companies or research organizations in cooperating. A potential partner may be reluctant to enter into cooperation for a variety of reasons. It may lack interest in the product, process or application in question, or the timing may be wrong. For example, a user who has recently invested in new equipment will rarely require a new solution immediately (but the need may arise some years later). Other reasons for a lack of interest can be that the counterpart is already cooperating with sombody else, or prefers to work alone, thereby assuring full control over the development process. The former problem is not seldom met by Swedish firms trying to establish cooperation with foreign customers or suppliers. Frequently these are already committed to collaboration with domestic partners.

Secondly, there may be difficulties in establishing a functioning and effective technical exchange. For example, a large geographical distance and differences in language, culture or personal characteristics may constitute a barrier to efficient communication. Naturally the risk that the cooperation will be disturbed by such factors is greatest when the partners are situated in different countries. This explains why technical cooperation seems to take place between domestic partners to such a great extent (see e.g. Håkansson & Laage-Hellman, 1984). If the parties fail to establish a fruitful exchange there is a high risk that the cooperation will be broken off without having produced the desired result. In the extreme case the whole development venture might be jeopardized.

A third danger is that cooperation with one unit may preclude cooperation, or even business exchange, with others. For example, a process user may reject cooperation with a certain equipment supplier if he knows that the latter has a close relationship with a competitor. The reason can be the user's fear that his own process know-how will be spread to the competitor via the supplier (the chemical industry is sometimes said to be rather secretive for this reason). On the whole the risk of losing control over proprietory technology may be one reason to refrain from external cooperation.

Development interaction thus offers both opportunities and difficulties to the individual firm. Some of these will be illustrated in the following sections where we shall present some results from a study of the Swedish special steel industry.

Process Development in the Swedish Special Steel Industry - some Results from an Empirical Study of Technical Exchange between Companies

Purpose and design of the study

A strong commitment to R&D has always been a distinctive feature of the Swedish steel industry. It holds a technically leading position in several product areas such as stainless steels, bearing steels and tool steels. Over the years a number of new, innovative processes and products have been developed in Sweden. A common denominator for several of these is that they have come about as a result of cooperative R&D ventures. This observation was the starting point for a current study of the Swedish special steel industry. The principal empirical purpose is to describe and analyze the technical exchange between the special steel producers and their customers and suppliers. The theoretical framework is the interaction and network approach outlined in Chapter 1. Based on an interaction model we are investigating process and product development cases where two or more units have been involved. At the current stage we have concluded 10 cases. Three of them deal with new metallurgical processes, the others with product development. The cases come from three of the five major special steel groups which comprised the main part of the Swedish special steel industry at the time when the study began (1981).[6]

The cases have been selected in order to illustrate different ways in which a steelmaking firm can make use of external resources in its process and product development. By interviewing technical and marketing managers we have for each case collected data on the technical exchange between the focal steel firm and the counterparts with which it has interacted in a certain situation. Some aspects of the interaction process that we have tried to cover are: the background and purpose of the interaction, the pattern and content of the technical contacts and joint development activities, the organization of the cooperation and the external units' importance for the outcome of the project. Two of the three process development cases will be described and analyzed below. But before so doing, we shall take a look at the network within which these developments have taken place.

The Swedish special steel industry and the process technology network

Steel is commonly divided into two categories, viz. commercial steels and special steels. The former are often defined as unalloyed steel containing less than 0.6% carbon and only minor amounts of other elements. By definition all other types of steel are special steels. They normally contain one or several alloying elements, such as e.g. chromium, nickel, molybdenum, tungsten and cobalt. Unalloyed carbon-rich steels, bearing steels, stainless steels, high speed steels and hot work and cold work tool steels form some of the more important product groups. The manufacturing process is often complicated and requires advanced equipment and substantial technical know-how.

Today special steels comprise about one third of Sweden's total crude steel production. In comparison 5-10% is the typical figure for most industrialized countries. In terms of value special steel accounts for 60% of the output. The main part is exported directly through the steel firms' own worldwide networks of sales subsidiaries and agents. In addition there is a considerable indirect export in the form of engineering products.

By tradition the Swedish special steel industry has specialized in the production of products for special uses which require very high quality. Some examples of typical end-products are ball bearings, saw blades, milling cutters, razor blades, watch and valve springs and stainless tubes for power stations and chemical plants. The competitiveness has to a large extent been based on advanced technology, and a strong commitment to R&D has therefore always been a characteristic of the Swedish steel industry. It has for example been very amenable to new and improved methods of production. As we shall see, Swedish metallurgists have themselves made several valuable contributions to the advance of steelmaking technology.

The present study deals primarily with process development which took place in the 1960s and 70s. In Figure 2:4 we have tried to illustrate the process technology network during this period as seen from the perspective of the Swedish special steel industry. The figure identifies the principal Swedish units and gives some examples of important foreign units. The kind of relationships which exist within the network are not shown but will be discussed below.

Besides the steelworks the most important categories of unit involved in the development of special steel technology are suppliers of process equipment, raw materials and operating supplies, and different types of research organization. Some independent technical consulting firms are also members of the network but seem to play a marginal role in new process develop-

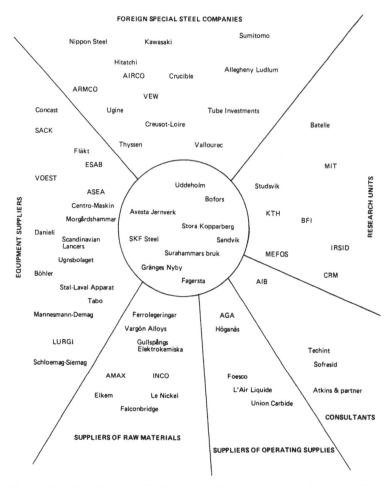

Figure 2:4. The Process Technology Network as seen from the Perspective of the Swedish Special Steel Industry (the situation during the 1960s and 70s).

ment. Their role is rather to participate in the international transfer of technology.

As shown in the figure the nine major special steel companies in Sweden during the 1960s and 70s were Avesta Jernverk, Bofors, Fagersta, Gränges Nyby, Sandvik, SKF Steel, Stora Kopparberg, Surahammars Bruk and Uddeholm. In total they operated some 25 steel mills. Since then the industry structure has changed substantially as a result of the worldwide steel crisis that occurred in the late 1970s. Today the special steel production is dominated by three big groups - Avesta, Sandvik and SKF Steel. The first two specialize in stainless steel while SKF is the main producer of high carbon and low alloyed special steels.

Among the Swedish suppliers ASEA and Morgårdshammar have long been the most important units from a process development point of view. ASEA manufactures metallurgical process equipment, process control systems, and other electrical equipment for the steel industry. In certain fields, such as ladle metallurgy and hot isostatic pressing, ASEA undoubtedly is a world leader. Morgårdshammar has specialized in fabricating rolling mills for bars and wire rod and is one of the leading international suppliers in this field.

The two important research units are MEFOS and the metallurgy section of the Royal Institute of Technology in Stockholm (KTH). MEFOS runs two pilot plants, one for process metallurgical research set up in 1965, and one for metal working research, instituted in 1975. Various types of 'development companies' may be active in fields which are of relevance to the special steel industry. Studsvik Energiteknik is one such company. In spite of the high standard of the Swedish process metallurgical research, contacts with foreign research units are also important sometimes. The Massachusetts Institute of Technology (MIT) can be mentioned as an example of a prominent university with which Swedish steel companies have had contacts. Pilot plant research institutes similar to MEFOS exist in several countries. Three of the best known in Europe are IRSID in France, CRM in Belgium and BFI in West Germany.

To conclude, the Swedish special steel companies can be seen as members of a worldwide process technology network consisting of firms and research institutes engaged in the development of special steelmaking technology. More or less strong technological linkages exist between different units in the network. In the following section we shall see how some Swedish special steel companies have established technical cooperation with other members of the network.

Developing new steelmaking processes through cooperation

As suggested above the Swedish special steel industry has old traditions within the field of process metallurgy. Large resources have been invested in process development, and over the years this has resulted in a number of more or less significant process innovations. Several of these, such as e.g. the Kaldo process for oxygen steelmaking and the technique for inductive stirring in electric arc furnaces, have attracted great international attention and been adopted by foreign steelworks in different countries.

A common feature of several of the more significant special steelmaking innovations is that they have come about as a result of close cooperation between different steelworks and ASEA. ASEA is a major producer of heavy electrical equipment and one of the flagships of Swedish industry. High R&D intensity and technology-based competitiveness have always been the hallmark of ASEA. In the course of its 100 year history it can boast several pioneer accomplishments within several technological fields. Already in the late 19th century ASEA helped to start the electrification of the Swedish iron and steel industry, which at that time was one of the world's leading exporters of high-quality steel. In 1927 ASEA formed its Furnace Department in order to be able to meet the increasing needs for electrical furnaces of the expanding Swedish metallurgical industry. In close collaboration with its domestic customers ASEA has since then developed into a leading international supplier of furnaces and other electrical equipment to the metallurgical industry. As a matter of fact many of its main products have been developed in direct cooperation with Swedish steelworks. The best known example is probably the ASEA-SKF process, a refining method which produces very pure steel and increases the capacity of the melting furnaces. It has become a big commercial success. At present some 50 ASEA-SKF units have been installed in steelworks throughout the world. This development venture is a good illustration of the importance of close contacts with qualified, demanding users. Without the cooperation with one of SKF's steel mills, the practical development of the ASEA-SKF process would not have been possible (Bengtsson, 1983).

The development of the ASEA-SKF process was also of great importance to SKF. By providing a cost-efficient method of producing clean steel it helped to strengthen SKF Steel's position in the world market for high quality bearing steels. It is true that the competitors have been able to buy the process from ASEA, but being first undoubtedly gave SKF some years' start. SKF

Steel has long followed a clear strategy of technological leadership in process technology. By further improving the ASEA-SKF method and developing other processes, partly in cooperation with ASEA, SKF has continued to increase the efficiency of its steel production.

Another excellent example of what can be achieved when the resources and skills of two companies are combined within a seller-buyer relationship is the development of the ASEA- STORA process. This case will now be described in detail from the perspective of the innovating steelworks. Another case dealing with the development of the ASEA-NYBY process, will then be reported. Each of the two cases will be commented upon and analyzed from the viewpoint of the interaction and network approach.

Case: The ASEA-STORA Process

Introduction

On June 17th, 1970 one of the major news items in the Swedish newspapers was the announcement of a new revolutionary steel-making process. In a press conference the previous day the two companies Stora Kopparberg and ASEA had disclosed that they had jointly developed a new powder metallurgical method, called the ASEA-STORA process (ASP). It was primarily intended for the production of high speed steels, which is a class of very highly alloyed tool steel used in the manufacture of various types of cutting tools, such as twist drills, hobs, broaches, gear cutting tools and saw blades.

In 1970 the process was only at the pilot plant stage but Stora Kopparberg announced its decision to build a full-scale plant at the Söderfors works where the headquarters and main production facilities of its special steel division were located. Now, 15 years later, we can conclude that the investment has proved to be a technical and commercial success for the Söderfors works[7]. However, the development was far from straightforward. A great deal of hard work and perseverance has been necessary in order to pursue the project all the way from the first preliminary ideas in the mid 1960s to the establishment of a stable and profitable business. In this case 'the ASP story' will be described from the very beginning up to the mid 1970s when the running-in of the first ASEA-STORA plant was completed. Of course the development did not stop there. A continual process and product development has taken place ever since, but these activities are not covered by the present case.

The ASEA-STORA process consists of two major steps. In the first one a fine steel powder is produced by atomizing molten steel. This takes place in a high chamber through which steel droplets are allowed to fall. By the time they have reached the bottom they have solidified. The powder is then poured into cylindrical capsules made of ordinary steel plate which are subsequently sealed by welding. The second major step consists of cold and hot isostatic pressing of the capsules into an absolutely compact, non-porous steel. The compacted capsules, which thus constitute the output of the ASP plant, are worked conventionally by forging and rolling to the desired dimensions.

General background

In the mid 1960s, when the first ideas leading to the ASEA-STORA process were first discussed, the technical development in the high speed steel (HSS) area was mainly concerned with the development of new, preferably more highly alloyed, grades. The objective was to achieve greater hardness and thereby longer tool life. It was well known that the poor metallographic structure in HSS limited the tool performance, but the structure was considered difficult to influence. By changing the solidification conditions (e.g. the size and shape of the ingots) and introducing new hot working procedures the steel producers tried to improve the structure, but with only modest success. Later in the 1960s electro-slag refining was applied to HSS production but this did not lead to any radical improvements in the steel properties either.

Most development of the new alloys was taking place in the USA. The driving force was the introduction of new high temperature materials in the aircraft engine industry. These materials were difficult to machine and therefore required better tools. In the automotive industry, the biggest user of HSS tools, very little happened in those days. In the majority of applications conventionally made standard HSS grades were sufficient. The machine-tool development had not yet influenced the materials development. But later, at the beginning of the 1970s, significantly improved gear cutting machines, where the tool was obviously the weakest link in the system, began to appear.

Apart from these general trends in the development of conventional HSS some attempts to apply powder metallurgy (P/M) had been made in the USA and Europe. Most of these projects were based on conventional P/M technology for manufacture of sintered iron products or somewhat modified processes[8]. But the technical problems had proved enormous and already in the mid 1960s most of these projects had been discontinued without having left the laboratory stage.

In Söderfors a broad range of special steel products was produced in those days. The Söderfors works was also a pioneer in the manufacture of cemented carbide products. These were produced by a powder metallurgical technique similar to that used for sintered iron products. HSS and other tool steels constituted a relatively small part of the total tonnage in the mid 1960s, but toward the end of the decade they were the cornerstone in the product program.

The first ideas

In May 1965 a young metallurgist named Per Hellman was engaged as research engineer. During the fall he discussed different possibilities of using powder metallurgy with the former R&D manager who had recently left Söderfors to become professor at one of the Swedish institutes of technology. The latter, who was engaged as a consultant, was an eminent powder metallurgist. He had certain ideas based on classical P/M technology. One of his ideas was to press and sinter a mixture of iron powder and other metal powders made of the different alloying elements in HSS (tungsten, molybdenum, vanadium, etc.) and thereby fabricate HSS tools directly from powder. However, Per Hellman did not believe in the proposed method, although he was attracted by the idea of using powder metallurgy. He explained:

My idea was that we should make HSS with a different metallographic structure. How we did it didn't matter! The important thing was that we should get a better structure and then many of the problems would be solved. The fact is that it was a generally accepted belief that the structure was the strength limiting factor of HSS tools.

Since I was aiming for improved properties I thought it was unwise to use the classical approach. We knew that others had tried to do that and had failed. Of course we should press and sinter, that was the only method I knew, but we should only make an intermediate product in that way. Then we should forge or roll in order to eliminate all the residual porosity. In other words I did not believe in the idea of making finished tools directly from powder.

I had also decided from the very beginning that we should use pre-alloyed powder with the final steel analysis. Atomization of molten steel was then the only powder manufacturing method available.

When I started I knew nothing about either HSS or powder metallurgy. Maybe that was an advantage! Because if you know something about a field you are inclined to use that particular bit of knowledge. That was what many others did. But for me it was different. As I was ignorant of both fields I could more easily think freely.

It is interesting to note that almost exactly at the same time Crucible Steel in the USA began work on an almost identical process from the same starting point. But the Söderfors people of course did not know about that. Indeed it was not until around 1970 that they learned of it.

The process is taking form

In the early 1966 Per Hellman started to experiment in order to check the feasibility of the idea. A simple equipment for water atomization was constructed at the Research Centre of Stora Kopparberg's steelworks at Domnarvet. The pressing and sintering was done at the laboratory of the cemented carbide factory in Söderfors. The availability of these two facilities was important as it meant that the project could be run at very low cost.

Examinations of small pieces of steel showed that the structure looked good, but there were several problems. One of the most important was the extremely high oxygen content which resulted from the use of water atomization. A great deal of effort was devoted to the solution of this problem. After a while gas atomization was tested as one possible solution but the equipment was not well suited to this purpose. By and by Per Hellman came to the conclusion that what he needed was inert gas atomization carried out in a closed chamber so that the powder could be protected from oxidization. He did not know of any industrial application of this technique. In January 1968 a decision in principle was made that a possible new plant should be based on argon atomization.

During the same period Per Hellman happened to read in a technical magazine about the High Pressure Laboratory of ASEA in Robertsfors. In the early 1960s ASEA had developed a new type of isostatic press, called QUINTUS presses, initially intended for fabrication of industrial diamonds. Within ASEA's Industrial Division a separate department was formed with the responsibility for marketing ASEA's equipment and know-how within the high-pressure field. A special laboratory equipped for pilot plant research on cold and hot pressing of powder was established in Robertsfors a few years later. *When I read about ASEA's fantastic apparatuses up there I understood that hot isostatic pressing was the right way to do the powder compaction. It was absolutely necessary for us to obtain a completely dense, non-porous product*, Per Hellman said.

Shortly after the decision to use argon atomization had been reached, 0.5 million Swedish crowns was requested to build and run a pilot atomization plant in Söderfors. Per Hellman decribed the situation as follows:

> *From the beginning of 1968 I was finally aware of what I exactly wanted. My problem was to sell the idea internally. Up to that point the project had not claimed much money but now there was a need to invest. The process already existed in principle but it was not possible to make progress without testing it practically on a larger scale. Somebody had to start producing high quality inert gas atomized powder. It was therefore of vital importance to get this half million crowns.*

It was a fairly large sum in those days and the request was rejected. But Per Hellman did not give up. He continued to work on the project although he did not feel much support from his surroundings.

The first contacts with ASEA

In early 1968 Per Hellman approached ASEA for the first time and proposed some form of cooperation. The ASEA people reacted very quickly. In particular the sales manager of the QUINTUS Department immediately understood and personally invested a great deal of effort in the project.

The QUINTUS presses were unique, sophisticated equipment, but the problem was that very few realized how they could be used. ASEA had begun to realize that instead of just selling an apparatus they should offer a whole package including equipment and process know-how. ASEA was therefore interested in a close cooperation with Stora Kopparberg. Per Hellman commented:

> *It was very easy to establish a cooperation with ASEA. We had almost identical interests, as we were both interested in developing a complete process. Of course my goal was to produce steel with a new method while they saw the opportunity to sell the method. But we both knew that we had to develop the process first.*

The pilot plant phase

As part of his 'campaign' to obtain money for the project Per Hellman looked more closely at the economy of the new process. He was greatly helped by the ASEA people who on their side studied the compaction part. However, despite favourable cost calculations the management was still reluctant to invest more resources in the project. But in summer 1968 an opportunity arose when Bo Berggren, a former fellow student of Per Hellman, was appointed new general manager of the Special Steel Division. Per Hellman presented the case to him and took him to the High Pressure Laboratory where ASEA performed an excellent demonstration. Bo Berggren was enthusiastic about the project and in January 1969 the board of directors decided to build the pilot atomization plant.

It took six months to erect the plant. From summer 1969 to March 1970, when the investment decision was made, a very large number of trials were carried out. As it had taken such a long time to obtain the money all was well-thought-out and carefully prepared. The purpose was first to produce material and prove that it was possible to make tools with improved properties. Secondly, it was necessary to decide on the process data. What pressures, temperatures and times should be used during the powder pressing? How should the gas nozzles and other details of the atomization equipment be designed? etc.

It was a very intensive period. Previously it had been more or less a 'one man project'. Per Hellman was now appointed head of a new department for long-term materials research. *But we only worked with processes!*, he commented. Powder was produced in the atomization plant. Specially made capsules made of mild steel were then filled with powder and sealed by welding. The capsules were sent to Robertsfors where they were isostatically pressed by ASEA. Forging and rolling were ultimately performed at the Special Steel Division's plant in Vikmanshyttan where there was suitable production equipment for processing of small batches. Each company paid for their own part of the development activities.

The testing of different process parameters in the pilot plants constituted a basis for specifying the requirements for a production plant in terms of equipment sizes, capacities and characteristics. The scaling-up was sometimes difficult as such a plant had never been built before. For example theoretical calculations made by a consultant indicated that the atomization chamber should be over 25 m high. Such a tower would be extremely expensive and make the whole project unfeasible. On the basis of practical experience from the pilot plant a lower height was chosen. As it was in most cases impossible to carry out large-scale tests many uncertain decisions of this kind had to be made.

Parallel with these trials ASEA worked on the design of the compaction equipment. The fact was that ASEA had only made small presses for laboratory purposes before. Now for the first time it must build large-scale presses for an industrial application. This called for new technical solutions in several respects. ASEA therefore had to make an extraordinary development effort, primarily in the form of brainwork and designing. A very large number of highly qualified engineers from different departments were involved. *I don't know how many worked on the project, but I had contacts with a whole crowd of people,* Per Hellman said. Already at an early stage it was agreed that ASEA should also build the atomization plant. However, all the technical specifications and drawings were in this case prepared in Söderfors.

The characteristics and properties of the produced material were extensively tested in the laboratory by metallographic studies and simple standardized turning tests. The results indicated that the structure was perfect, and it should be possible to improve the tool performance as predicted. A small quantity of the steel was also given to a tool-maker who manufactured a series of twist drills and tested them under shop floor conditions in his own testing laboratory. No details about the new material were given to the customer. He was told only that the steel company had developed a new grade which it wanted to have tested. The results proved to be very favourable for the new steel.

The investment decision

The results obtained during the fall were considered so encouraging that an investment request for a production plant was drafted during the first months of 1970. The new division manager, Bo Berggren, actively canvassed the board of directors, and on March 12th the decision was made to invest. The finishing negotiations with ASEA started immediately and the contract was signed one week later.

In connection with the purchase of the production equipment it was also decided to buy a pilot press. It was anticipated that many production problems would arise. Experiments in the big plant would be rather expensive and it would therefore be better to have a pilot press where different process parameters could be tested. A complete pilot plant was also needed for the future product development.

The cooperation agreement

Two months after the purchase contract had been signed ASEA and Stora Kopparberg also made a cooperation agreement concerning the process. In order to be able to sell the complete process it was essential for ASEA to gain access to the patents and know-how regarding the atomization, which were entirely in the hands of Stora Kopparberg, and the future production experience. The QUINTUS people realized that the latter was much more important than the mere right to sell the process.

Stora Kopparberg had two reasons to reach a formal agreement. First there were certain economic advantages. Stora Kopparberg would, for example, receive a royalty for each ASP plant sold by ASEA. The second reason was that Stora Kopparberg thought that it would be impossible to keep the technology for itself. If the process proved to be good enough competitors would certainly find some way of evading the patent regulations. It was therefore considered better to sell the technology. They would thereby learn of other producers several years in advance and be able to adapt. The competitors were expected to recognize the advantage of buying the whole process from ASEA instead of developing it from the very beginning.

In describing the role and importance of a formal cooperation agreement Per Hellman said:

> *For the key persons involved there is really no need for a formal agreement. As a matter of fact there was not a single word written between us until most of the work had been done. During the first period all was based on the enthusiasm of two individuals. It is true that without a common interest and a desire to accomplish something together a written agreement is worthless.*
>
> *Another thing is that a formal agreement might be useful in order to avoid misunderstandings and to solve minor problems, especially when two big companies are involved. Many people are affected by the project and it is necessary that those who are on the periphery know which rules are valid.*

One can say that the agreement involved an assurance that at some time in the future Stora Kopparberg would not prevent ASEA from pursuing its strategy of selling complete processes. The open and trusting atmosphere between the two companies was built on personal relationships. If these persons disappeared the current positive attitudes could possibly be changed. In that case ASEA would at least have secured certain minimal rights.

Production start and running-in

During the two years following the investment decision and up to the start of production the pilot plant trials continued intensively.

The testing of different process parameters resulted in increasing certainty regarding the design of the production plant but successively different dead-lines were reached where the definitive technical specifications had to be settled.

In June 1972 the first full-size capsule was compacted. Very soon various technical problems related to the equipment appeared. This was not surprising as the technology had never before been applied on a large scale and under production conditions. But it was impossible to foresee exactly what problems would arise. Let us take the compressor of the hot isostatic press as one example. Since the capsules were pre-heated when charged the pressure had to be pumped all the way up to 1 000 atg (the laboratory presses were charged with cold capsules). This required the use of very sophisticated membrane compressors that before had only been used in laboratories. At the beginning the membranes frequently broke down which led to constant production disturbances.

After some time, when it became apparent that the running-in problems were greater than predicted and that they would not be solved without a massive contribution from ASEA, a joint project organization was formed. There was a central project group with the overall responsibility for solving the equipment problems. It consisted of a dozen persons representing different functions in the two companies (production, engineering, maintenance, process development, materials research, etc.). Under this group there were about 10 different sub-groups of technical specialists which worked on well defined technical problems. The central group held meetings every 3-4 months, but besides that there were many informal contacts. The sub-groups met very frequently, usually once a week, which was possible thanks to the geographical proximity.

Some problems were solved partly in cooperation with subcontractors, as e.g. in the case of the above-mentioned compressor, which had been supplied by a French firm. Other problems were for practical reasons solved without external cooperation although ASEA was well informed about the course of events.

In early 1974, i.e. 1 1/2 years after the start of production, the most serious problems had been solved, and the ASP plant worked satisfactorily although there were still some difficulties to be overcome in order to attain a perfect production reliability.

The project organization remained until spring 1975 when it was formally dissolved. From time to time internal task forces were later formed to cope with special production problems.

Market introduction

After the announcement of the ASEA-STORA process and the investment plans in 1970 the company began to prepare the buyers for the market introduction by distributing small quantities of test material produced in the pilot plants. Because of the major production problems encountered after the start-up of the full-scale plant in 1972 the sales of ASP steel were however not pushed very hard.

As mentioned above it was not until 1974 that the plant could steadily produce larger quantities of ASP steel with a high, even quality. From that year the company tried to launch the product to a broad range of customers through its marketing organization in Sweden and abroad. But sales still developed very slowly in spite of the excellent properties. Because of the high price and the different property profile compared with conventional HSS the ASP products had to be marketed in a completely different way. In fact it took the company three years to learn this lesson and to develop a suitable market introduction strategy. An important component of this strategy was the establishment of so-called 'three party cooperations' with selected tool makers and end-users. The aim of these cooperations was to develop tool applications where the ASP steel led to improved cost-efficiency for the end-users. Since 1977 the marketing has been successful and in 1980 the production capacity of the existing plant had to be extended in order to meet the increasing demand.

Some concluding remarks

In describing ASEA as a partner in the ASP-project Per Hellman expressed the following viewpoint:

> *I have never met a company where there are so many techni-cally skilled people. It was of crucial importance that ASEA placed all these engineers at our disposal in order to solve problems. It doesn't go without saying that they should have done that. ASEA was doing so many things!*
>
> *It was very easy to cooperate with ASEA. I think that one*

of the reasons is that we were equally dependent on each other. Both parties realized that they could not make it alone. Nobody had the advantage over the other, so to speak. A prerequisite for successful cooperation was also a respect for each other's competence. All these things can never be replaced by a written agreement. It is easy to fulfill an agreement literally, but it is never enough. You have to do something more in order to produce something really good.

The close contacts with ASEA have been maintained since the termination of the running-in phase, although there have been no joint development activities. The Söderfors works continues to buy spare parts and when the capacity was expanded a significant part of the order sum went to ASEA. It has been considered valuable to have a continuing technical exchange with ASEA due to its great technical competence and leadership within the high pressure field.

'The ASP story' is a good illustration of the escalating difficulties which a company may encounter in the course of an innovation process. The invention was the easiest thing to make, the process development was more difficult, to make the process function on a large scale was still more difficult, but the most demanding task was the market introduction.

Analysis of the ASEA-STORA Case

In Chapter 1 we outlined a network model including three basic classes of variables, viz. actors, resources and activities. The actors are the companies, departments or individuals who perform activities or control resources (either directly through ownership or indirectly through relationships with other actors). The resources, in the form of physical, financial or human assets, are used by the actors when they perform activities. The latter may be of two kinds. Transformation activities, such as manufacturing or internal R&D activities, are always carried out under the control of one actor. Transaction activities, on the other hand, aim at transferring control over a resource from one actor to another. The selling and buying of goods and technical cooperation are examples of typical transaction activities.

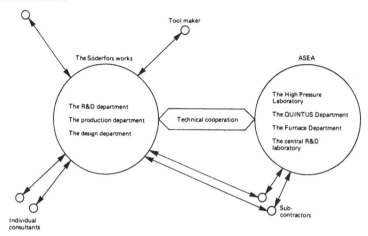

Figure 2:5 Main Actors Involved in the Development of the ASEA-STORA Process.

We shall now use this model to analyze the ASEA-STORA case. The purposes are to reach a better understanding of what has happened in the case and to illustrate how the model can be used to identify opportunities and problems in technical cooperation within networks.

Even though several units were concerned in the development of the ASEA-STORA process there were two main actors at the firm level, the Söderfors steelworks and ASEA. This is illustrated in Figure 2:5. Within each of the main actors several different organizational units were involved. As we have described in the case study it was also possible to identify a few key actors at the individual level.

The first important point we can observe is that the two firms, at the time when the cooperation began, were performing parallel activities, which could well be combined. ASEA had earlier developed the QUINTUS press to be used for the manufacture of synthetic diamonds. ASEA had however withdrawn from that market and was actively searching for other applications of its high pressure technology. These activities had not yet led to any concrete results when the opportunity to start cooperation with Söderfors arose. Those responsible at the QUINTUS Depart-

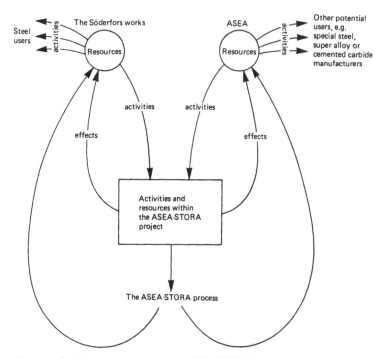

Figure 2:6 Main Features of the ASEA-STORA Case.

ment had realized that they needed process know-how if they
were to be able to sell the equipment. The contact with Söderfors
therefore gave a welcome possibility to develop a first industrial
application. Söderfors had encountered technical difficulties in
their own development activities. The QUINTUS press of ASEA
offered a possible solution.

The two actors thus had a common interest in developing a
new steel process which included ASEA's high pressure technology. The driving forces were the potential marketing opportunities of steel and equipment respectively. But the two actors not
only had goals which partly overlapped. They also had matching
resources which, if combined, could produce synergy effects in
the development work. From a resource point of view the two
actors formed a strong constellation.

The basis of establishing a joint development project was thus
very good. But this did not suffice to guarantee a successful
outcome. A functioning, effective cooperation can ensue only

from the appropriate performance of the different transformation and transaction activities. A suitable division of work must be agreed, the R&D activities performed by the different actors coordinated, the technical exchange between the actors organized, etc.

It seems that it was relatively easy to establish cooperation notwithstanding that no relationship existed at the beginning. It is true that ASEA and Söderfors had done business with each other before, but the individuals involved had no prior experience of their opposite numbers. ASEA's QUINTUS Department and High Pressure Laboratory were new units. There are several factors explaining why the cooperation was so free of problems.

An important factor was of course the geographical location of the actors. Both companies are Swedish and the distance between Söderfors and Västerås, where ASEA's headquarters and most of its facilities are situated, is rather short. This facilitated the personal contacts, which were crucial especially during the pilot plant and running-in phases when engineers in the two companies were working closely together on the same problems.

Other studies which we have carried out have shown that four conditions normally have to be fulfilled if two actors are to collaborate fruitfully (Håkansson *et al.*, 1983). These conditions are that the actors should:

a) have a common 'language'
b) have mutual knowledge of each other
c) have mutual trust
d) make great demands upon each other

All these conditions seem to have been fulfilled in the ASEA-STORA project.

The actors naturally communicated in Swedish which of course facilitated the information and social exchange. But the 'language' is not only a matter of Swedish, English, French, etc. In order to understand each other the individuals involved need to use a common terminology and have a similar way of thinking in technical questions. These conditions are normally fulfilled if the individuals have a similar cultural and educational background. The 'language' question does not seem to have caused any problems in the present case, but in other contexts we have found situations where the 'language' constituted a major obstacle to efficient technical exchange.[9]

In order to assure a functioning development relationship the actors involved also need knowledge about each other. For example, they need to know the skills and resources of the counterpart, how he is organized, and which persons should be approached in different matters. To build up this knowledge takes time and demands human resources. In fact it can only be acquired by interacting with the counterpart. The frequent, broad personal contacts between the personnel of ASEA and Söderfors which were made possible by their closeness, the two companies' large human investments in the project and the chosen mode of organization (joint project groups) probably contributed to the build up of mutual knowledge.

The establishment of mutual trust is very important in R&D cooperation. The use of new knowledge always involves risk. The outcome can never be guaranteed as unpredictable difficulties always crop up in the course of the development work. Both parties must be able to trust that the counterpart is serious and 'puts all his cards on the table'. The mutual trust is also a prerequisite for the freedom of the information exchange.

In the case of the ASEA-STORA project we can see that the trust was built up, as is often the case, through an interaction process where the two companies developed the cooperation in a step-wise manner. They started on a small scale (meetings, demonstrations, preliminary calculations, etc) and then successively escalated their commitment. Even though there was no prior relationship to build upon the experience of similar cooperative ventures within the network probably facilitated the establishment of a trustful relationship. As we have mentioned earlier other departments within ASEA have pursued several successful cooperative process development projects with Swedish steelworks. Even Söderfors had participated in such cooperation.

As regards the individual level we can conclude that two of the main actors, Per Hellman in Söderfors and the sales manager of the QUINTUS Department, also seem to have collaborated very well.

The advantage of having demanding customers is often mentioned. It forces the supplier to do its utmost to satisfy the requirements of the customer[10]. In the present case both the supplier and the customer had high technological ambitions which pervaded their cooperation.

In Figure 2:6 we have tried to summarize the main features of the case. We have two actors which by coordinating their resources and activities within the frame of a joint project succeeded in developing a new revolutionary steelmaking process. The effects on the two actors are related to the technical end-result as well as the cooperation itself. The establishment of a close relationship was thus an important result *per se*. It gave the actors access to external resources which could be useful in activities other than the ASEA-STORA project. Even though the two actors had common goal of developing the new process the effects of the project were somewhat different for each.

For Söderfors the main result, of course, was the ASEA-STORA process in terms of both plant and process knowledge. This was an important resource which could be used in its marketing and manufacturing activities directed toward the steel users. The introduction of the ASP steel with its excellent properties undoubtedly led to the strengthening of Söderfors' position as one of the world's leading suppliers of high speed steels. Besides the acquisition of knowledge the establishment of a relationship with ASEA gave Söderfors a certain access to external competence which could be useful in the further development of the technology. A by-product was the possibility of obtaining royalty income on ASEA's future sales of the entire process or parts of it.

For ASEA the cooperation project first of all led to the sales of a complete ASEA-STORA plant to Söderfors. However, more important in the long run was that it gave knowledge useful in the further marketing and development activities directed toward other potential users of the powder technology. They not only learnt how to design and build large-scale isostatic presses, but also acquired knowledge and experience concerning other parts of the powder metallurgical field (e.g. powder manufacture by inert gas atomization). Moreover they gained indirect access to patents and production experience through the relationship with Söderfors.

Thanks to its own knowledge base and the cooperation agreement with Söderfors, ASEA was enabled to market the whole ASEA-STORA process to other steelworks. Up to now only one complete plant has been sold (to the Soviet Union). On the other hand, a fairly large number of large QUINTUS presses have been sold to other types of customers, e.g. to producers of super alloy parts for the aero-engine industry. The Söderfors plant was a valuable reference plant in this connection. Thanks to the location close by and the good relationship it was easy for the QUINTUS people to take their customers and prospects to Söderfors.

The knowledge gained in connection with the ASEA-STORA project not only resulted in immediate marketing opportunities. It also constituted a base for further technical development. ASEA has continued to develop new types of equipment and processes within the powder metallurgical field. As we shall describe in the next section the ASEA-NYBY process for stainless steel tubes was developed together with Gränges Nyby. The STAMP process is another powder metallurgical method developed in cooperation with Surahammars Bruk. The possibility of carrying out pilot plant and large scale tests in Söderfors was used especially during the first years following the completion of the ASEA-STORA project. Later on ASEA built up its own facilities and, as mentioned above, developed cooperative relationships with other steelworks.

In Chapter 1 we put forward three main arguments why technological innovation should be seen as an interaction process between several actors in the network. These pertained to knowledge development, resource mobilization and resource coordination respectively. The present case sheds light above all on the resource coordination argument. Neither of the two companies would have been able to develop the process alone. It was only by coordination of specialized resources controlled by different actors that the ASEA-STORA process could be brought about. The importance of resource mobilization is also illustrated. Thus, the solving of certain critical problems required a massive mobilization of ASEA's highly qualified, but limited, R&D resources.

We can conclude that this is an example of an extraordinarily successful cooperation. The outcome was very rewarding for both parties, and there seem to have been very few problems with regard to the cooperation itself. But what would have happened if the two companies had not come together or had failed to establish a fruitful cooperation? We can only speculate, but it is reasonable to believe that both companies, sooner or later, would have found somebody else to cooperate with. Söderfors for example could have chosen another method for compacting the powder. Maybe ASEA would have found another company having a similar process development problem where the QUINTUS press could be seen as a possible solution. The establishment of a technical cooperation might have been more difficult, but in one way or another the development efforts would probably have gone forward. We know that the result would have been different for both ASEA and Söderfors, but we cannot tell whether they would have been better or worse off.

Case: The ASEA-NYBY Process

Introduction

The ASEA-NYBY process for manufacturing seamless stainless steel tubes was developed during the 1970s by the Swedish special steel producer Gränges Nyby (in the following called 'Nyby'). The process is based on a powder metallurgical technology, which had not previously been used for seamless tube production. It consists of four major steps:

1. Powder manufacture by inert gas atomization
2. Manufacture of powder-filled capsules
3. Cold isostatic pressing in a QUINTUS press
4. Hot extrusion to the required shape

Large-scale production began in summer 1980 and about one year later Nyby had wholly abandoned the conventional manufacturing method.

Licences for the ASEA-NYBY process can be acquired from Nyby in conjunction with the purchase of process equipment from ASEA. A first licence agreement was signed in 1981.

How the project started

Since the beginning of the 1960s the market growth rate for seamless stainless steel tubes has been very low, almost zero, primarily because of increasing competition from welded tubes. The improved quality of the latter has made it possible in many applications to substitute welded tubes for seamless tubes, which are more expensive to produce. This trend, which was reinforced during the 1970s, has led to increasing price competition and falling profit margins especially for the standard type grades. At the same time, however, the demand for special tubes made from the more highly alloyed grades has increased. As a result the seamless tube producers have gradually switched their production toward an increasing share of these more advanced grades.

Gränges Nyby was a medium-sized producer of extruded seamless stainless tubes. Its production process was not totally integrated. The rolling of the bars to be extruded was done by other Swedish steelworks on a contract basis. When Nyby changed over to the more highly alloyed grades, it began to encounter increasing production problems due to the lack of control over the entire manufacturing process. As a result they started to look for alternative routes of production. Large-scale trials were made with some existing techniques, such as electro-slag refining and centrifugal casting, but these methods did not fulfill Nyby's requirements for a new method:

–lower production costs than the current method
–no increase in capacity
–flexible production and the possibility of manufacturing various types of highly alloyed stainless steels.

One of the potentially most interesting ideas which was studied was a powder metallurgical method similar to the newly developed ASEA-STORA process for fabrication of powder high speed steel. But instead of using hot isostatic pressing Nyby's process was based on extrusion of pre-compacted capsules.

The idea of using powder metallurgy was introduced by Christer Åslund, who was responsible for the investigations of alternative tube production methods. He had come into contact with powder metallurgy some years earlier while working at the Royal Institute of Technology. He had some contacts with the Söderfors steelworks. By coincidence he had also been in touch with a small Belgian firm making stainless steel powder for other purposes. Talks with this company had produced certain useful ideas.

From 1973 to 1975 Nyby investigated the possibilities of using powder metallurgy parallel with the work on the other alternatives. The first step was to study the economy of stainless powder production and the possibility of achieving a satisfactory powder quality. Christer Åslund travelled around and visited different metal powder producers, mainly in the USA. These were in general fairly candid as they did not compete with Nyby. Small batches of stainless powder were purchased, and simple experiments undertaken to test the process and measure the material properties obtained. The results showed that inert gas atomized powder was to be preferred from a quality point of view.

After three years of preliminary investigations on a small scale the basic features of the process were thus defined and patent applications could be submitted. However, a large amount of intensive development work remained in order to work out the details of the process. In 1975 it was therefore decided to start a development project with Christer Åslund as project leader.

The development phase

In early 1976 a large quantity of stainless steel powder was bought from an American super alloys producer. Large-scale trials were then conducted over a period of 3-4 years for which some financial support was given by STU. One of the most important objectives was to test the process to such an extent that a statistically valid judgement of the production reliability could be made. It was known from the preliminary tests that the idea worked but there were many problems with regard to several of the process stages. For example the capsule design, the powder filling and the sealing of the capsules proved to be critical issues. Considerable efforts were made to solve these problems.

Extensive material investigations were also undertaken to ensure that the properties were as good as or better than those of seamless tubes made by conventional methods. The tests showed that substantially improved mechanical properties could sometimes be achieved, e.g. in the case of the new types of ferritic stainless steel. Owing to the uniform, fine structure of powder metallurgical products the resistance to certain types of corrosion could also be improved. But the principal advantage of the process was still considered to be the lower production costs, especially for the highly alloyed grades.

At the same time as the large-scale trials started, Nyby also invited offers from different equipment suppliers. It was obvious from the outset that ASEA would be chosen as supplier of the powder manufacture plant and the isostatic press. Thanks to the close cooperation with the Söderfors steelworks ASEA was the only equipment supplier with experience of building a large-scale inert gas atomization plant for steel powder. ASEA was also the leading supplier of isostatic presses and the only one with experience of building large-scale presses operating at the extremely high pressures in question. The availability of ASEA's equipment was thus a prerequisite for the project as such. *Without ASEA there would have been no process,* Christer Åslund concluded.

At the outset Nyby considered ASEA as 'a pure equipment supplier' and revealed little information about the new process. ASEA on the other hand was initially perceived to be rather sceptical to the idea. In the course of time, however, the contacts were gradually intensified, and many discussions ensued regarding the technical specification of the equipment to be offered. But there was never any 'real development cooperation' between the two companies. The chosen isostatic press was a standard press in ASEA's program. On the powder manufacture side ASEA had already built one atomization plant, but the new plant had to be scaled up and adapted to stainless steel. This work was done by ASEA based on the fixed specification. Nyby was thus little involved in these activities, but the ASEA people on their side had some cooperation with the Söderfors works where certain ideas were tested.

While the development and design of the powder manufacture plant could be left to the supplier to a great extent, the development of the capsule manufacture, filling and sealing steps required a great deal of development work on the part of Nyby. As a matter of fact the capsule line was the most important and novel part of the process. From the beginning Nyby worked on this problem together with a Swedish welding company, which, however, was unable to suggest a satisfactory solution. In this situation Nyby decided to approach Volvo's Olofström works. They knew that Olofström was very skilled in designing various types of welding lines and had a large technical staff working thereon. The first contact was made during 1976 and Volvo and Nyby subsequently developed and designed the new capsule line in close cooperation. The Volvo engineers worked out different solutions, which were subsequently tested at Nyby, then redesigned, tested again, etc. Step by step the solutions were approved by Nyby and the line thus successively evolved. The experimenting and designing continued even after the purchase decision had been reached in order to make a line at sufficiently low cost. Christer Åslund was very satisfied with Volvo's contribution: *The importance of our cooperation with Volvo cannot be exaggerated. They were technically competent and were very alert.*

The investment

During the winter of 1977 the management of Gränges Nyby had come to the conclusion that they wanted to invest in an ASEA-NYBY plant (except for the extrusion press which already existed). The development work had advanced so far as to prove that the process worked and that the material properties were good. There were also offers for the equipment and economic calculations which showed the profitability of the investment.

Financing was the major problem. The steel crisis had seriously affected both Nyby and the parent company and no money was available. However, in May 1978 Nyby received a government loan and the construction could begin. Two years later, in April 1980, the plant was ready to come into operation. In the summer of the previous year Nyby had merged with a part of Uddeholm and a new company, Nyby Uddeholm, had been formed. This merger caused many problems due to the subsequent re-organization and thereby delayed the start by six months.

From January to August 1981 the newly formed Powder Products Division under the headship of Christer Åslund worked on the running-in of the ASEA-NYBY plant parallel with a successive closure of the conventional production. The running-in of the atomization plant was facilitated by the fact that Nyby had become a part of the Uddeholm Group which also included the Söderfors works. Through the contacts with Söderfors it was possible for Nyby to acquire know-how regarding the operation of the powder plant.

Since the fall of 1981 the seamless stainless steel tube production of Nyby has thus been fully based on powder metallurgy. In November Christer Åslund concluded that the powder manufacture and capsule line functioned well but that certain problems in the extrusion press still remained to be solved. He estimated that the running-in should be completed within six months.

Market introduction and further development

It is always difficult to introduce new steel products when there is only one supplier. Nyby has realized this problem and in most cases has refrained from pushing the 'powder tubes' as being better than conventional tubes. Many small customers have not even been told that the tubes are made from powder. On the other hand, the advantages of the 'powder tubes' have been stressed to the 20 largest customers. Extensive field tests have been carried out together with several of these customers, normally large chemical firms, and the result has been positive as a rule.

The market introduction has however been delayed by the fusion between Nyby and Uddeholm. The whole sales organization, including the foreign subsidiaries, has been subject to radical changes which of course has disturbed the selling activities. The introduction of the highly alloyed grades, which are used in more demanding applications, are particularly problematic. In addition, as a result of the merger, a substantial part of the standard products has disappeared from the delivery program, which has forced Nyby to search for new customers within the more advanced application fields in order to increase the sales volume to a reasonable level. One of the advantages of the ASEA-NYBY process is the possibility of producing extremely highly alloyed grades economically. But the potential to develop new types of alloys, where the composition is optimized with regard to the powder metallurgical technique, has not yet been utilized. Christer Åslund said

If we had had the resources we should have started long ago. But because of the crisis we have been busy with other problems. It was a question of survival!

Much of the more long-term material development work stopped when the research laboratory at Nyby disappeared. The product development has now started again. Even if it is

still of a relatively short-term character it is evolving in the right direction.

When Nyby decided to go ahead with the investment it was agreed that the new process should be marketed by ASEA to other stainless steel producers. In conjunction with the purchase of equipment from ASEA, know-how should be offered to the customer through the signing of a licence agreement with Nyby. The two companies should accept joint responsibility for the transfer of know-how and the training of personnel.

The first licence agreement was signed in the fall of 1981 with the French steel company Vallourec. At the beginning Vallourec would buy ready-made powder filled capsules from Nyby and process them further in its existing extrusion press. According to the plans, it would later purchase powder from Nyby which currently had an overcapacity in its atomization plant. For Nyby this also meant an opportunity to develop a technical and commercial cooperation with a new partner. Especially in the marketing field Nyby saw a potential for future cooperation.

Analysis of the ASEA-NYBY Case

The units involved in the project

The ASEA-STORA case was an example of close cooperation between two firms. The interesting feature of the ASEA-NYBY case is rather that it illustrates how one firm (Nyby) interacted with several external units in the course of a major new process development project. Figure 2:7 shows the principal units involved.

The external units were used or engaged by Nyby for varying purposes, and the interaction with them occurred during different phases of the project. During the idea generation phase contacts with other powder manufacturing firms (e.g. Söderfors and the Belgian company) contributed to produce useful ideas. During the development phase both ASEA and Volvo played key roles. The access to Söderfors' production experience facilitated the running-in of the atomization plant. During the market introduction of the new powder tubes, application tests were carried out

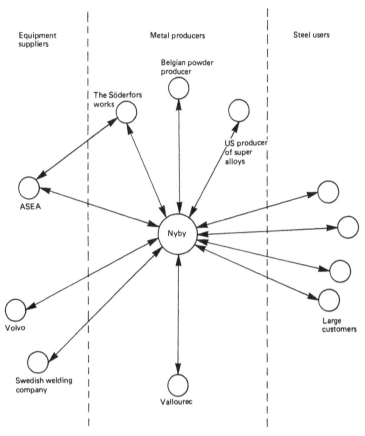

Figure 2:7 External Units Involved in Nyby's Development of the ASEA-NYBY Process.

together with certain large customers. In the marketing of the process technology itself Nyby cooperated with ASEA. Through the establishment of a relationship with Vallourec new marketing and development opportunities were created. The technical exchange took place not only between Nyby and its different partners. In the development of the atomization technique ASEA had certain direct contacts with Söderfors.

Dependence on other actors

We shall try to analyze the case with the help of our network model. First we can conclude that the development activity as

74

such was initiated by a lack of control over certain production activities (the rolling of bars to be extruded). Nyby wanted to acquire full control over the entire production chain and therefore needed to develop a new method for producing the tubes (given the internal conditions! Nyby was a relatively small producer; a cost-efficient production method existed but it required a much larger tonnage).

As in the preceding case the innovating steelworks was strongly dependent on other actors to achieve its goal. Without the pre-existence of certain external resources and activities performed by other actors the whole process idea would not have been feasible. Thus, ASEA's earlier development of the ASEA-STORA process together with Söderfors was essential for the development of the ASEA-NYBY process. It is also important to note the importance of closeness. If the ASEA-STORA process had been developed in some other part of the world, e.g. in the United States, it would have been more difficult for Nyby to obtain information about what was going on. The technical risk would have been greater if key resources had been controlled by unknown actors far away. In this case Nyby had long standing contacts with both ASEA and Söderfors which facilitated the establishment of a technical exchange.

To develop the process Nyby not only needed contacts with qualified equipment suppliers. It also had to obtain a large quantity of suitable stainless steel powder to use in the trials. Such powder was not available within the country. Nyby had to go to the USA where they found a super alloy producer who was willing to supply the powder.

The interaction with ASEA

ASEA's role during the development phase was more as 'technology supplier' than an equivalent partner in a joint venture (compare with Figure 2:3). But, as hinted above, ASEA was undoubtedly a key actor because it had already developed solutions which could be used, and controlled R&D resources which could serve to provide new solutions. At the outset the relationship between ASEA and Nyby was rather limited and 'business minded'. It seems that neither party had full confidence in the other. Nyby perceived that ASEA did not believe in the process idea and feared that ASEA was only interested in acquiring

Nyby's knowledge. As a consequence the information exchange was somewhat restricted at the beginning. But by the time the process began to take shape and the individuals involved learned more about each other a trustful relationship could be built up between the two firms. This illustrates, as we concluded earlier, that the establishment of a functioning technical cooperation often takes some time and demands human resources. The need for such relationship-specific investments is one reason why it is much easier for most firms to cooperate with domestic than with foreign partners.

The interaction with Volvo

Nyby's cooperation with Volvo has interesting aspects from a network point of view. Nyby had worked on the capsule line together with another Swedish supplier. The latter was well established in the welding area, and it was natural to turn to this company. However, when these activities did not lead to the desired result Nyby started to consider other partners. They knew that Volvo-Olofström possessed interesting skills which had been acquired through activities in another network (automobile manufacture). Nyby therefore approached Volvo and initiated a close cooperation with them. This is interesting because Volvo was definitely not an established supplier to the steel industry. To find a partner which had the necessary resources to solve this critical problem Nyby was thus obliged to go outside 'the natural network'. But it should be noticed that these search activities did not start until 'the natural partner' proved wanting.

Effects on the actors

In the previous case we saw that the project had important consequences for both of the two main actors. In this case the process user seems to have benefitted most from the joint activities. By interacting with several other companies Nyby could mobilize the necessary external resources and produce a range of multicompetence effects in the development work (see Chapter 1). Furthermore, the establishment of relationships with ASEA and Volvo allowed Nyby to create coordination between its own and their specialized resources.

The effects on the other actors were probably not equally

decisive for their long-term development. ASEA was already established within powder matallurgy. But, naturally, the Nyby order constituted an important event which gave a valuable opportunity to further develop the existing technology and acquire new experiences. Later on the cooperation between the two firms was broadened to include other powder metallurgical processes.

As regards Volvo-Olofström the participation in the development of the ASEA-NYBY process gave an immediate delivery order and additional experiences from a new application field. The project represented one development step in the external exploitation of its welding line knowledge. They can be sure to become a supplier in connection with eventual future sales of ASEA-NYBY plants. But because of the small market potential for such plants the principal long-term value probably consists of the knowledge which was acquired in the project.

Concluding Remarks

To conclude this chapter we should like to emphasize three striking aspects of technical development in networks. These have to do with the resource dimension of relationships and networks, the timing of different activities and the long-term, uncertain character of the innovation process.

Let us start with the resource aspect. As illustrated by several examples successful process development is to a great extent associated with the ability to use resources in the surrounding network. This holds good for both process users and equipment suppliers and research institutions. The already established relationships constitute valuable 'resource channels' which facilitate the mobilization and coordination of complementary resources controlled by different units. As a matter of fact close cooperation between equipment manufacturers and qualified users is often a prerequisite for successful development of new, innovative processes.

Occasionally companies may need to supplement these 'nearby' resources by establishing new relationships with 'more distant' units. These can be geographically distant members of the same technology network or members of a completely different network. In both cases the company goes outside the natural set of cooperation partners. It can be an advantage that these units have a different approach from the predominant one. It can lead to the generation of new, interesting ideas, but to advance further these must be integrated with activities and resources in the existing network. Thus, it might be easy to generate ideas but the achievement of a commercialized product or process often requires large investments over a long period.

To summarize, we believe that cooperation within the old, well-known relationships is extraordinarily important for technological development. However, from time to time it is necessary to involve outside units in order to renew the innovation process and create the conditions for major new advances in the technology development.

Good timing is a prerequisite for successful technical cooperation. The willingness of a certain counterpart to enter into cooperation is very much dependent on the phase in which he finds himself. The development of the ASEA-STORA process is an excellent illustration. Both parties were in a similar situation which made it easy to establish a close cooperation. In the case of the ASEA-NYBY process ASEA was not very interested at first. This indicates that the timing was not perfect when the process idea was presented. In order to find 'the right partner' a company may therefore need to go out and discuss with many firms. Alternatively it can change its own time planning and wait for a potential partner to be prepared to enter into the project. The great importance of timing as a condition for technical cooperation is further illustrated by the following example, viz. PREMID (Programmable REMote IDentification) which was initially developed in the 1970s by the Institute of Microwave Technology in Stockholm and later taken over by Philips Elektronikindustrier in Sweden. PREMID was an innovative product which *inter alia* opened up new possibilities in production control and materials handling. The Microwave Institute wanted to develop applications for the automobile industry and therefore searched for cooperation partners, primarily among the Swedish manufacturers. But neither Volvo nor Saab were interested because they had recently invested in other systems for identification of car bodies. Instead the Microwave Institute established a cooperation with BMW in Munich which was on the point of building a new assembly plant. As BMW's philosophy was to offer a great degree of customization the PREMID concept fitted in very well with their investment plans. In the meantime Volvo and Saab have become ready to invest in new systems and interested in testing PREMID.

Timing is also important in relation to the whole network. If a new process idea is to be well received the idea has to fit in with the activities current in the network (compare with the PREMID example). If it is introduced too early it can be difficult to gain access to the necessary resources due to a lack of interest on the part of the other members concerned. In the extreme case these may even actively oppose the idea. Conversely, a new process may arrive too late. This may happen, for example, if another process has recently been introduced and reached a certain spread. Then the introduction of the new process might be a hopeless task even if it offers potential advantages to the would-be users. Those who have already built a plant do not have an immediate need of a new process. And those who are planning to invest often prefer a well-tried solution, especially in the case of a large capital investment. This problem was faced by e.g. Uddeholm and Creusot-Loire when they tried to sell licences for their jointly developed CLU process for stainless steel refining (see Laage-Hellman, 1984, Appendix 3). In spite of potential cost savings compared with the competing AOD process the commercialization of the CLU process failed. One main reason was that a large number of AOD units had already been installed and, as a result, the amount of production experience under various operating conditions surpassed that of CLU. Thus, the cost benefits were not big enough to justify the investors in taking the risk of choosing the relatively untried CLU instead of AOD.

Technological innovation can be characterized as a long, complicated and uncertain process. New production processes, as well as new products for that matter, can seldom be developed in a straightforward way. Companies are more likely to be involved in a number of different development activities the outcome of which is very uncertain. Some of these lead to the expected result, but most of them lead to something else. The question is then what to do next, given the acquired experiences and the available internal and external resources. The company therefore always has to act from the starting point of what has happened earlier. In other words technology development is a kind of trial-and-error process where flexibility and adaptability to changing conditions are key elements. And to succeed the innovating company needs a great deal of perseverance. Take the ASEA-STORA project for example. Each time a development stage had been completed new, unexpected problems arose. To go ahead it was necessary to initiate new activities and engage new resources within or outside the company. In certain situations, such as e.g. when the ASP steel was to be introduced onto the market, it was even necessary to search for new partners not previously involved and establish cooperation with them.

If maximum use is to be made of the development efforts individual projects or activities thus have to be put in a larger context. An activity which is judged a failure in one context can often be turned into a success by applying the knowledge in some other field. For example up to now ASEA has only sold two ASEA-STORA plants. This is not very much considering the large resources which have been invested in the process. If it were not for the spin-off effects the commercial and economic outcome of the ASEA-STORA project would probably not look too good.

To summarize, perseverance is one of the most important prerequisites for successful technological development. Innovating firms need great perseverance in order to be able to devise a technology which is adapted to the network, and to convince other members of the network to participate in the development.

Given these three aspects of technological innovation it is almost invariably impossible to make rational and certain judgements of development projects in advance. The outcome of a particular project or activity will to a great extent depend on how other actors act, and the resulting interaction between the different actors. As a consequence it is in general very difficult to pursue a clear-cut R&D strategy toward radical innovation based on specific project selection criteria, quantitative financial evaluation methods, etc. Instead a more 'opportunistic' approach is called for. If the company seeks to be a leader in process technology it should act in such a way as to become exposed to many innovative situations. This can be done by pursuing internal R&D activities within certain areas of interest to the company and interacting in various ways with other units. This will produce opportunities to create interactive and multicompetence effects and to mobilize and coordinate resources. But the external interaction should always be based on the firm's own long-term technology strategy, i.e. in what areas it wants to have its skills in the future. This 'functional limitation' should constitute the starting point for all cooperative R&D ventures.

It is important to note that external interaction is resource demanding in itself. Like the internal R&D capacity the company's capability to interact is also limited. Therefore it is generally impossible on each occasion to take advantage of all the cooperative opportunities to which the company is exposed. It has to choose a certain limited number of partners and develop long-term cooperation with them. A less extensive technical exchange can take place in parallel with other units in the network. If these exchange situations create new, more promising opportunities to innovate there might be reasons to question the choice of partner. But due to the long-term nature of the innovation process and the investment character of relationships the partners should not be changed too often. Otherwise there is a risk that the R&D results, even though technologically interesting, will never lead to commercial and economic success.

The partner choice, if on the whole we can talk about a conscious decision thereon, should thus be governed by long-term considerations. Moreover, the heterogeneous character of the actors and their resources makes it theoretically impossible to make an optimum partner choice from a resource point of view. The result produced by a certain constellation of actors depends as much on how the resources are combined as on the resources as such. It is implicit that the cardinal issue is not to find 'the optimum partner' from some technologically rational point of view, but rather to find suitable partners with which the company can develop over a longer period.

Notes to Chapter 2

1. As pointed out by Porter (1983) the great power of technology as a competitive variable lies in its ability to alter competition through changing industry structure.
2. Von Hippel has studied the sources of innovation in some high-technology

industries. He found that a 'user dominated' pattern of innovation predominated in certain industries while in others a 'manufacturer dominated' pattern prevailed. He maintains that the former is typical for many industrial goods. On the basis of his own findings and others reported in the literature he has proposed a 'customer-active idea generation paradigm'. He hypothesizes that this paradigm better fits the conditions typically prevailing in industrial markets than the traditional 'manufacturer-active paradigm'. The latter is feasible in the case of consumer goods but generally offers a poor fit to the requirement of industrial product idea generation (von Hippel, 1978).

3. The aim of the study was to increase the knowledge of the mechanisms for dissemination of information and research results. For this purpose six of STU's programs for knowledge development were investigated in detail. The other five were Electronic and electro-optic component technology, Information processing, Industrial food processes from a nutritional point of view, Cellulose-fiber-based materials technology and Wood materials. In total we interviewed more than 60 researchers at universities, research institutes, and industrial firms.

4. One can hypothesize that the role distribution is partly a result of the interaction pattern developing in the network. According to this line of thought the establishment of relationships between certain units leads to the creation of specific roles for these units. The role played by an individual firm is thus dependent on the specific units with which it interacts. For example, one firm meeting strict and far-reaching requirements from its customers is likely to develop a different role compared to a competitor who is serving less demanding customers. This hypothesis will not be further developed in this book but could well be the starting point for an empirical study.

5. The choice of cooperation strategy in R&D is discussed in Håkansson & Laage-Hellman (1984). They make a number of propositions regarding how internationally operating companies should act given certain firm-specific and network-specific factors.

6. Preliminary results are reported in Laage-Hellman (1984).

7. In 1977 the Söderfors works was acquired by Uddeholm. Since 1982 it is part of Kloster Speedsteel AB, a company which was formed by merging the high speed steel divisions of Uddeholm and Fagersta.

8. Conventional P/M technology implies pressing of iron powder to a pre-shaped body and subsequent sintering to obtain a relatively dense product. Because of the residual porosity sintered products have low strength and are therefore used in applications where a cheap product is wanted and the strength is not a critical property.

9. Scientific and technological development often means language development in one form or another. But the reverse case, that language development also means knowledge development is not always true. Jargon is frequently used to hide a lack of knowledge. Apart from this problem we can conclude that new languages are often difficult to learn. Generally it is not enough to listen. The receiver also has to learn how to use the language and, sometimes, continue to develop it further. This requires investments in both time and motivation.

In our study of the six STU programs we found that the language could be a barrier to efficient communication particularly within the information processing network. The concept and language development is extremely rapid which not only makes it difficult for the academic researchers to communicate with the practitioners in the companies. Frequently the researchers cannot even understand each other.

10. Glete (1984) has shown that the high technological level of ASEA, LM Ericsson and several other Swedish high-technology companies is to a great

extent the result of long-term technical cooperation with qualified, demanding Swedish customers.

In a comparative study of the machine tool industry in Great Britain and West Germany Parkinson (1982) examined the view that the poor performance of British manufacturers could be related to the relatively low technical sophistication of their domestic customers. The findings indicated that West German buyers were significantly more likely than their British counterparts to stress technical factors rather than economic factors when purchasing new capital equipment. Furthermore, West German users were more demanding of innovation and appeared to play a more active role in the product development process. Parkinson therefore concluded that in order to improve the performance of British manufacturers of machine tools, and other engineering products, greater attention should be paid to changing the domestic users' approach to adopting new technology.

Chapter Three

PRODUCT DEVELOPMENT IN NETWORKS

Håkan Håkansson

The Importance of Studying Product Development

Product development has received substantial attention during the last two decades. There are hundreds of studies and articles devoted to models, analyses, and recommendations regarding this concern. However, the main body of research concerned with product development has been criticized for applying an overly narrow perspective - see for example Gold (1979) and Teubal (1979). The aim of many studies has been to attempt to isolate and analyse individual phenomena instead of relating the development issues to broader and more general processes or structures. The law of reductionism has been applied.

This can be explained, at least partly, by the fact that the research has been oriented towards a specific actor - usually the producer - which has been seen as the innovator. The 'Newton Syndrome' was in other words operative here. Another explanation is theoretical which we will come back to later.

The high level of interest for product development can largely be explained by two interrelated factors. One of these is the increased professionalism among managers leading to a belief that companies can and furthermore need to be managed by some kind of central unit. Taking this perspective new products have been seen as the means to secure the future of the company. During the strategic wave of diversification this interest was especially strong. The second and interrelated factor is a belief that everything is developing more quickly, implying an increased uncertainty and, among other things, shortened product life cycles. Thus, as a consequence there is an increased need for the continual development of new products. It will not be discussed here whether these two factors are based on solid empirical ground or are simply beliefs. This is, however, an interesting question with no self-evident answer.[1]

Thus, our interest in product development is not based on arguments such as a lack of earlier studies or that this issue has become more important for management. Instead our argument is that product development must be looked at in a new way.

Before presenting our view we will briefly describe earlier studies. It is possible to categorize the studies of product development in a number of different ways - for recent reviews see Kennedy (1983) and Golding (1983). Taking a network analysis perspective it is interesting to see which actor is perceived to take the initiative in product development. For example, is it the producer, the user or some other actor? These perspectives are examined further in the following three subsections.

Product development initiated by the producer

The overwhelming majority of studies focus on the producer as the initiator of the product development process and a lot of attention is devoted to determining new methods to increase the success rate of new products or at least reduce the failure rate. The reasons for this concentration on the producers is related to the two earlier mentioned factors - active management and increased degree of change. This focus is so established and self-evident that, for example, the previous mentioned review articles (Kennedy (1983) and Golding (1983)) take it for granted[2].

The main conclusions from all these studies are recommendations to producers to use a rational, straight-forward product development process. The process consists of a sequence of activities such as information gathering, screening, business analysis, product design, market test, and commercialization. During the whole of this sequence the producer is believed to take the initiative and, for example, make the external contacts that are necessary. Much is said about actions and very little about reactions.

Product development initiated by the user

A few studies have perceived the user as the active party. Von Hippel's studies are the most well-known, but there are also others, e.g. within the field of industrial purchasing. Von Hippel (1978) and (1982) has developed a 'customer-active' paradigm which he contrasts to the old 'manufacturer-active' paradigm. His main argument for this new paradigm is that it better suits

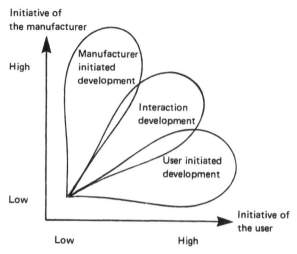

Figure 3:1 The Initiator of Product Development.

(a) industrial buying behavior, and (b) the engineering problem-solving process. The customer-active paradigm is supported by empirical studies of, for example, semiconductors, electronic sub-assembly processes, and scientific instruments.

Results showing the same tendencies can also be found in certain industrial purchasing studies (see for example Axelsson & Håkansson (1984)). And it would be very surprising if such was not the case, since users such as GM, Toyota, General Electric, Volvo, IBM and others, who are themselves large manu-facturing companies, invest heavily in product and process effi-ciency.

Product development as an interaction process between users and producers

In the preceding sections the initiative has been seen as located in one actor only. An alternative is to combine these two and see both the producers and the users as taking an active part in interaction processes. In the IMP-study (Håkansson ed., 1982) company case analyses revealed that in a majority of situations joint development activities could be identified. Several other examples, as well as empirical data, were presented in Chapter 1 of this book regarding these interaction processes.

The three types of product development studies that we have described are complementary but to some extent also over-lapping as is shown in Figure 3:1. Together, they should cover the whole spectrum of product development but as will be seen in the next section serious criticism can be directed against all of them.

Product Development in a Network Perspective

One criticism toward the main body of earlier research regarding product development is, as was mentioned ealier, its focusation on one or a few actors. If we, for example, consider the three groups of studies described in the previous section, the first two are oriented toward one specific type of actor and the third to the interplay between two actors. Thus, in all these studies the focus has been restricted to very few actors with accompanying types of analysis variables.

It is also possible to identify a theoretical explanation associated with how the relationship between individual events and the total technical development process is perceived. If the total technical development is believed to be composed of a lot of small and independent events then it is perfectly correct to study individual events or factors in an isolated way. But there is an interesting alternative. If the individual events are simply indicators or expressions of the total technical development process then there is a need to use an approach that takes as its starting point the total process. A number of studies have tried to do this in different ways. For example, Utterback & Abernathy (1975) relate individual events to the product life cycle, Baranson (1978), who studies the development within a whole industry, Sahal's (1980) study of technical development as a learning process, and Stindl (1980) who perceives it as an evolutionary process.

In this chapter the network perspective outlined in Chapter 1 will be used as a tool to relate individual events such as product development to the total technical development within some technical fields. The network constitutes the frame to each individual episode but is at the same time built up by these episodes.

The network perspective, in accordance with the model in Chapter 1, means focusing on relationships between actors, activities and resources. In the network perspective a specific product becomes a question of relationships. It itself constitutes a relationship between certain activities, resources and actors. A product is produced through certain transformation and transaction activities - and is consumed through others. Some resources are used when it is produced or during the transactions and others when it is consumed. Some actors control these activities and resources. Thus, a product relates these activities, resources and actors to each other in a specific way.

In this way product development becomes a network issue in terms of how the new product will affect the activities, the resources and thereby the relationships between the actors. The response is furthermore related to how this new product is connected to other types of change that occur at the same time within the network. It can not be isolated from other technical changes nor from economic or power structure changes. In summary, individual product development activities must be seen as part of a total technical development process which in turn must be regarded as an integral feature of the specific network.

Technical development as a combined political and random process

In order to obtain a better understanding of the total technical development process we have to start with the network. Several network features, which are important to the technical development process, were described in the first chapter. These can be summarized as follows:

1) The existence of activity cycles and transaction chains. Different activities are systematically related to each other and constitute repetitive activity cycles which in turn are combined to build up transaction chains. The repetitiveness is important as it is a prerequisite for efficiency. The border between different activities is always arbitrary and can be changed.

2) The instability and imperfection of the networks. The terms optimality or balance can never be applied to a network as there is no single evaluation criterion or reference point. The role of the network is different for all its members and also in relation to all other networks con-

nected to it. Thus, there are always both possibilities and reasons to change it. Existing transaction chains can be developed, new ones can be created, and so on. A network is in this way always alive and adaptable. But, at the same time there is no guarantee whatsoever that the development is positive from, for example, society's point of view. There is no 'invisible hand' creating a situation of efficiency and health. Instead there are several 'visible hands' that try to create situations that are beneficial to themselves.

3) The network structure creates limitations. The technical changes that occur must be performed within a certain structure. The existence of activity cycles and the combination of activity cycles in transaction chains are built on certain fixed combinations of resources. Thus, the relationships between different activities, between the activities and different resources, and as such between different actors, are based on specific technological concepts. The latter are expressed in the combination of products and the use of products and must be considered as a feature of the network.

The network characterized by the above three features develops over time. The second feature gives the reasons and possibilities and the first and third the limitations and directions. Three types of technical change activities can be identified:[3] investments in real capital, day-to-day rationalizations, and product development. Investments in real capital include development of equipment or new production processes thereby changing the transformation activities. Day-to-day rationalizations are all those thousands of minor changes that increase the efficiency of the transformation, the transaction activities or the connection of those two types of activities. Product development, lastly, always means changes in the transaction activities and, at least to some degree, changes in the transformation activities. It is clear from the above description that there are close connections between these three types of technical development, and in many situations they cannot be clearly separated.

Together these three types of activities, performed by the actors of the network, constitute the total technical development process. This can be regarded as a learning (Sahal 1980) or as an evolutionary (Steindl 1980) process. It can also be regarded as a 'muddling through process' (Lindblom 1959). Lindblom uses this concept to characterize the method of formulating policies (which he regards as synonymous to decision-making). He writes:

> *This might be described as the method of 'successive limited comparisons'. I will contrast it with the first approach, which might be called the rational-comprehensive method. More impressionistically and briefly they could be characterized as the branch method and root method, the former continually building out from the current situation, step-by-step and by small degrees; the latter starting from fundamentals a new each time, building on the past only as experience is embodied in a theory, and always prepared to start completely from the ground up* (Lindblom 1969, p. 44).

Although the muddling through process was originally developed for the purpose of describing and explaining decision-making, it can also be used to characterise the total technical development process within a given network. The muddling through process indicates the simultaneous existence of consciousness and experience of the actors and the presence of random situations. Consciousness is present via the actor who more or less systematically acts in a purposeful way based on earlier experience. The random variable is due to the large possibilities of different combinations and the genuine uncertainty connected with consequences in the future. Let us take a closer look at these three characteristics.

Consciousness gives the actors a direction or purpose to try to do what is best in each situation, and they will always try even if the results of the previous steps have not been as expected. However, consciousness of the actors is restricted by the lack of capabilities to survey the network and to estimate consequences in more than just a few dimensions. The existence of consciousness is important in another way as it indicates that technical development is never neutral - it is always biased towards the interests of those involved. Technical development is therefore a political process.

Experience is an essential ingredient of the process. Obviously, the actors perform and evaluate activities in relation to their experience. But the actors are also sensitive to the existence of others' experience. If others have used a specific product for some time this can be seen as a reassurance in terms of aggregated experience. The accumulation of experience is by no means a simple or straightforward process. Experience gained in earlier unsuccessful projects can suddenly become vital in a new project. Other experiences that beforehand are perceived to be important inputs in a project can during the process prove to be of little or no value.

The random factor is due to the interplay between several actors, alternatives and knowledge. This means that it is not possible to predict which ideas will be realized nor which of these will develop into useful products or processes.

Some ideas - alternatives - are tried and some of these successively become the standard solution. The reason for this may not be that they are better from a technical point of view but more that resources have been mobilized to make them useful. An alternative might have been better but as no resources have been put into the development of it this will never be known. The random factor is limited by the existence of earlier investments in resources (plants, equipments, relationships). This limitation will be further discussed in the next subsection.

Network as a control mechanism

Both the consciousness of the actors and the random factor are integrated aspects of the network. The actors' perspective and thereby their consciousness, are often influenced by the network which logically relates different actors and aspects to each other. The structure of the network will also give the random factor a non-random (systematic) character. The structure of the network, thus, will act as a control mechanism of the development process. It makes certain changes easier and others more difficult. The resources are structured in relation to the network and they are more easily mobilized if the development is in accordance with the structure of the network compared to the case when the development implies structural changes. In summary, we believe that in order to understand the technical development process one must understand the network in terms of structure and processes.

Technical Development from an Actor's Perspective

In the previous section the technical development of a network has been discussed in general. Here the problems at the actor level - mainly companies - will be examined[4]. In other words, we will take an individual company as a starting point and discuss how the processes and phenomena dealt with in the preceding section will look from this actor's perspective; especially in respect to the company's product development.

One starting point is the actor's ambition to improve his position, and the various ways to do this. One way is to develop the product. The network can be used in a positive way but can also be a very important limitation factor. This will be further discussed in the following three subsections.

The network as an obstacle to change

The network consists of many relationships, as well as other types of interdependence relations. As we pointed out earlier, the product is one of these interpendencies. If a product is changed other relationships might also have to be changed. This can only be done at a certain cost. Thus, when dependencies have to be altered, this always entails the cost of such a change[5]. The most common types of dependency which may be obstacles are

–technical dependencies
–knowledge dependencies
–social dependencies
–logistic or administrative dependencies

Each of these will be discussed in more detail below.

Technical dependencies are due to the fact that individual products are used together with other products or within technical systems. Successively related products are developed to better fit together. In a mature technology this integration of products is usually quite extensive (Utterback & Abernathy 1975). In a study of 'the hydraulic network', we found, for example, that the fittings between valves, pistons and packings, despite the fact that they were produced by different companies, had developed in a very extensive way. To introduce a new product within such a network requires that the producers of complementary products adapt to the new product. All these kinds of fittings are important from an efficiency point of view but they are certainly obstacles to new products. A new product does not usually fit as well from the start; nor does it use the capabilities of the other products in such an extensive way as the old products do. Thus, it takes both time and great effort before a new product can merge into the network.

Knowledge dependencies occur because the user needs certain product knowledge in order to use a product. This knowledge must be spread within the buying company to all those coming in contact with the new product. How many these are and how difficult this is depends both on the characteristics of the product and the buying company. The time between the introduction of a product and the full use of all its features by a buying company can be quite long. During that period there can also be a need to dispose of old knowledge[6].

The network is a social construction and as such built upon social relationships between the actors. This creates social dependencies which are difficult to break into for new actors. The normal social process of groups in terms of values, norms, legitimization, etc, are relevant.

Logistic and/or administrative dependencies can also create problems for a new product. These types of dependencies have become more important during the last decades as companies have grown internationally. Production units united together into international groups are often exposed to different coordination attempts, such as standardization of components or raw materials.

The following case illustrates this point. Ten years ago the Swedish bolt company Bulten AB attempted to introduce a new range of bolt products called HIGRIP. This new type of bolt was featured by a new configuration giving better technical performance. Bulten realized from the beginning that they needed to cooperate with a tool manufacturer. This cooperation was easily established as the largest Swedish tool manufacturer Bahco AB is situated just 50 km from Bulten. In tests made by customers -

mainly car manufacturers - the new products gave better production results in terms of decreased costs for the tools, shorter production time per unit and increased quality of end-product.

However, the car manufacturers were still reluctant to buy the new bolts because they wanted to have at least dual sourcing of all products. As a consequence Bulten and Bahco approached Britool and GKN in the UK and Kamax and Hazet Werk in West Germany. Together these six firms formulated a cooperation agreement. Despite these network activities and the superior technical features of the product the endeavour failed. The main reason, according to the responsible manager at Bulten, was an important administrative/logistic dependency. As long as the cars with the new bolts are in the hands of the car manufacturer there are no problems. The problems arise as soon as the car is sold. It can be sold anywhere in the world; consequently spare parts and tools must be distributed world-wide. Furthermore, the storing of both the old and new version of bolts would be required for some 20-30 years (until all previously produced cars have been taken off the road). The international nature of the market in combination with the long lifespan of the end-product became obstacles impossible to overcome. Thus, a simple bolt has important dependency effects.

Together, the four types of dependencies can create strong barriers for new products. It is important for the individual actor to have a comprehensive and multifarious picture of these dependencies before launching a new product. They are also the main reasons why incremental development steps are more common than dramatic changes. The total strength as well as the distribution of these types of dependencies varies between different networks. We will come back to this variation later on in this chapter.

Network as idea generator and resource source

As described earlier, the network consists of a number of relationships between actors, activities and resources. But there are also a number of potential interdependence relationships. Usually the number of the latter type exceeds the number of the former. Each potential relationship can be regarded as a possibility. Each actor is furthermore a potential cooperation partner and in this way a potential resource source. Partners can be used both as a means of attaining ideas and to receive direct development assistance. Lastly, there are numerous ways to conduct cooperation. Together these factors often give rise to a large number of combination possibilities of ideas, partners and cooperation forms.

Potential relationships can exist between activities, actors and/or resources, between different networks or activities, resources or actors in one network and some other activities, resources or actors in another network. Thus there is no limit to the number of ideas.

A difficulty for the actor is to know if a certain product will be accepted by the network. The only way to find out is to test the idea on some of the actors. The interplay within the network can in this way be used as a means of evaluating ideas. Ideas which fit into the network will be more or less accepted and the others will be more or less rejected. It is important to notice the 'more or less' of both acceptance and rejection. The network is seldom so uniform that only one type of solution will be accepted. A certain differentiation will be retained because different actors mobilize in favour of different solutions. A completely new idea, however, will usually not be accepted because it often changes the entire network structure. Thus, a network consisting of actors from previously different networks has to be built around the new idea. This takes time and demands a lot of resources.

The existing network can be used in different ways; there can be cultural differences in this use as illustrated by the following case from a Swedish company in a high-tech industry. A new product idea had emerged in the marketing department from a relationship with a large customer. The marketing department put forward a proposal and the R&D department was asked to give an estimate of the time and resources needed for the development of the product. The R&D department answered that it would take 24 months and the cost would be one million Swedish crowns. The managing director realized that if the R&D department estimated 24 months it would probably take 36 months and that would be too long. The managing director asked a Japanese company if they could develop the product and if so in what time limit and price. The Japanese company replied that they could to it in 9 months and for three quarters the cost estimated by the internal R&D department. The company chose to buy from the Japanese company. But how could the Japanese company do it so much faster and at a lower cost? The managing director explained the difference in the following way:

When our R&D department made their estimation they thought of a completely new product. The Japanese company divided the new product into different technical functions and chose existing solutions for most of these. Then they directed their development resources towards the design of the remaining components. In this way they utililized the existing suppliers much more effectively than we did.

The Japanese company used the network in a much more effective way. But in this case the Swedish company adapted by using the Japanese company as a supplier! The important lesson, however, is that there are many reasons for utilizing the existing network in all possible ways in the development work. In some situations it can be done through the purchase of development, in others through cooperation and in still others by procurement of advanced products or systems.

Network as an information transmitter

The network can be regarded as a communication system. In a well structured network everybody knows what is happening. In a few hours news of a positive or negative event spread throughout the network. A less structured network is not as effective or fast, but nevertheless has a communication function.

The actor can use the network to spread and/or to collect information. The actor does not in this way have to have direct contact with all other actors. He can use the network as an intermediate. The information reaching different actors, however, is influenced by the structure of the network. The content is perceived in accordance with a network logic. Each link absorbs and distorts to some degree the information. The information is formulated in the language of the network which in turn is related to the basic technology and the structure of the network.

The network does not merely transmit information about events that happen within it, but also information related to other networks. This gives an individual actor an opportunity to obtain an understanding of what happens within a large number of technical areas, without having to invest in direct relationships with each of them.

Product Development within Networks - some Empirical Illustrations

Having discussed the theoretical implications of the network model, this section will be devoted to a presentation of two empirical studies that we have carried out using this theoretical frame of reference. Product development within a specific network will be analysed as an integrated part of the total technical development process. The analysis will be done in the following sequence.

1. Identification of the main actors within a network.
2. Characterization of their activities and resources.
3. Description of the technical development for each of these actors for a certain period in terms of:
   a) investments in real capital (plants, equipment, etc)
   b) day-to-day rationalizations (all the minor activities that increase productivity)
   c) product developments
4. Analysis of how the characteristics of the product development are related to the total technical development as well as to the characteristics of the network. The description includes many technical details which, however, must be known in order to fully understand the later analysis.

This sequence will be done for the wood-saw network and the results will then be compared to the results from the analysis of another network - the metal drill network.

The Wood Saw Network

A network identified in relation to a technical function - viz. wood sawing was investigated[7]. The network was found to include four main types of actor. The saw mills are the companies

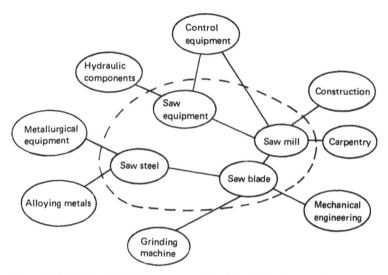

Figure 3:2 The Principal Structure of the Wood Saw Network.

that comply the function in order to produce a certain range of sawed wood products. They utilize equipment purchased from equipment producers and saw blades purchased from tool manufacturers. The equipment producers design and manufacture saw equipment such as band saws, circular saws and reductioners. The tool manufacturers produce saw blades of different kinds - blades for band, circular and frame saws - from strips or plates of steel. Lastly, the saw steel is produced by certain steel companies. These four types of companies and their suppliers and customers are held together by the fact that they are dependent on how timber and wood in general is cut in pieces. At the same time they can all influence how this function is completed. This network is illustrated in Figure 3:2 where some other indirectly involved actors are also indicated. Each of the four main types of actors will now be presented in more detail.

Saw steel producers

There were at the time of the investigation (1980-81) the following three producers of saw steel in Sweden; Uddeholm Strip Steel, SKF Strip Steel and Sandvik Steel. Sweden has a long tradition as a large producer of saw steel. For example, the Swedish companies have a world market share for wider strip saw steel of about 60%. The largest market is North America but the sales of the saw steel is spread throughout the world. The home market, as a consequence, consumes a small part (less than 10 percent) of the total production.

The saw steel is produced in the form of strips and plate. The steel must have a certain hardness and toughness in order to be effectively used in subsequent production steps. The problem is that these two properties are normally each others' opposite; thus, they are difficult to combine. These 'internal' properties are created by a special sequence of rolling and heat treatment. There are also requirements of the 'external' properties of the steel in terms of straightness and flatness. These properties are important as they facilitate the production of the tools. The production process is complicated, which as a consequence means long production time and high costs for resets. An important condition for efficiency is a certain volume of each production batch.

Tool manufacturers

This group of companies is in Sweden dominated by a few companies of which one has an international spread - Sandvik. The other have the Nordic countries as their major market. Among those are Westlings Sågbladsfabrik, Stridsberg & Biörk, Håkanssons, Munkforssågar and Brusaholms Sågbladsfabrik. The same type of industry concentration is also prevalent in other countries. For example, in the USA there is a handful of companies that dominates the sales of saw blades.

Usually, the tool manufacturers produce saw blades used by both saw mills and mechanical engineering companies. The production consists of operations such as stamping of saw teeth, setting or upsetting, and sharpening. The saw blades are straightened and if it is a band saw it must be put together in a welding operation. In some cases the teeth are coated with a special edge of cemented carbide or stellite. Certain of the tool manufacturers also service the saw units through resharpening used saw blades.

Most of the companies are small or medium sized family owned companies. They have different backgrounds. Several of them have their origins in steel production - e.g. Sandvik, Munkforssågar, and Stridsberg & Biörk. Others have originated closer to the saw mills - for example Westlings which started as a consulting company to saw mills.

There is a certain differentiation among the companies as they have specialized in different types of saw blades. Some specialize in circular saws, other in band saws, etc. The larger ones usually have a complete range of products.

Saw equipment producers

Saw equipment is produced by a very small number of companies in Sweden. The largest and the only one that markets almost the whole range of products is the state owned Kockums. This company has specialized in frame saws and reductioners. Circular saw equipment is produced to 75% by Ari AB and band saw equipment mainly by A.K Eriksson. Both these companies are middle sized, private owned companies. Besides these three there are a few smaller producers and agents such as CHE Johansson and Bröderna Lindqvist.

Basically there are three types of saw equipment: Band Saw, Circular Saw and Frame Saw. All three are mechanical constructions including a driving mechanism in which the saw movement is designed in different ways. The three types are substitutable but they have special features. Sweden was up to 1970 a 'frame saw country'. All the large saw mills had frame saws while the smaller and less sophisticated used circular saw equipment.

Saw mills

The saw mills are a very heterogeneous group of companies. In total there are about 2 500 mills in Sweden ranging from small simple farmer saw mills to highly automated saw mills within large company groups. The former usually sell their products to a local market while most of the latter export most of their production. In 1979 there were 44 mills with a production of at least 50 000 cubic meters.

A saw mill cuts the timber into different wood products. Sales go to the wood and construction industry. The former consists of, for example, house producers, carpentries, door and window producers, and cupboard manufacturers.

The main actors of the network have now been presented and the next step will be to describe technical development within each of them. The description is held on a general level and can be seen to regard some kind of typical actor in each group.

Technical development of the steel producers

Technical development will be described in terms of (a) investments in capital, (b) day-to-day rationalizations and (c) product development.

No large capital investments have been made in strip production during the last 15 years. However, a number of minor investments have been made in the production facilities. These have affected different stages in the production chain, especially control and quality inspection equipment. When making these investments some collaboration with suppliers of furnaces and rolling mills took place. Furthermore, greater investments have been made in the earlier stages of the steel production which for example was described in Chapter 2. The main effects of the investments both in earlier production steps and in strip production have been a more even and stable quality.

The day-to-day rationalizations have been important and are directly related to some of the above mentioned production investments as well as to attempts to change (limit) the product mix. The latter has been less successful. In general the day-to-day rationalizations have had as a goal to get a smoother and more effective flow of both production and product. This includes changes in transportation and storing.

The products have been successively improved through investment and day-to-day rationalization. Effects can be found in regards to internal as well as external properties. About 5% of the steel companies' turnover is invested in R&D but it should be taken into account that inspection and quality control are included in this figure. One change in the internal properties of the steel is that the purity has improved in terms of the amount of non-metallic inclusions. Changes in the external features have been better straightness and flatness which is important to the tool manufacturers as it decreases their production costs. This is especially the case for producers with high wage costs. The steel companies have in this way adapted to the customers in the Western countries as these have the highest wage costs. No major product innovation has occurred within the wood saw steel range. A new product, however, has been developed in regard

Table 3:1   Technical Development of the Saw Steel Producers.

Capital investments:	Minor investments regarding production and quality control equipment. Larger investments in earlier production steps at the steel mills.
Day-to-day rationalizations:	Important successive development of the production flow. Attempts to make product range limitations.
Product development:	Successive improvements due to the above made investments and rationalizations.

to the sawing of metals. The use of bimetal blades has been successful. The incremental development steps that have been taken have generally been done in collaboration with customers, mostly situated in the USA or West Germany. There have also been a number of cooperation projects regarding marketing activities between steel producers and tool manufacturers towards the saw mills. The technical developments of the saw steel producers are summarized in Table 3:1.

Technical development of the saw blade manufacturers

The producers have in general invested in new production equipment that has given faster and more automatic production as well as improved products. For example, this is so for TIG-welding of band saws and the successive improvements of the quality of the edges. Here a certain collaboration with producers of grinding machines has taken place. Also the punch equipment, which is the major piece of production equipment, has been improved.

Day-to-day rationalizations have been done in several ways. The most important change has been limitations of the product mix of individual tool manufacturers which in turn has increased the degree of specialization at the company level. However, as one of the tool manufacturers has learned, this process can go too far. The manufacturer decided to drop a whole section of saw tools (circular saw blades) 15 years ago, as it was deemed that this type of tool would loose market share in the future. In reality the opposite happened and the producer had to take up this type of product again.

The product developments have been limited and mostly re-

Table 3:2 Technical Development of the Saw Tool Manufacturers.

Capital investments:	More advanced production equipment in terms of automation and speed.
Day-to-day rationalizations:	Mainly product mix changes that have led to a higher degree of specialization at the company level.
Product development:	Edging of band and circular saws with teeth of stellite and carbide. Included more software (service) in the offers to customers.

garded the use of a special edge of carbide or stellite on the bands and circular saws. Furthermore, this has increased the possibilities for designing the latter in a more optimal way. Earlier the resharpening of the circular saw blades had changed the parameters such as the form of the tooth, distance between the teeth, and number of teeth. Now, when using special edges these parameters are stable and can be designed in a better way. Some of the producers have developed a package offer to the customer by adding services such as maintenance, resharpening and stocking. This has in some cases become more of a complete service offer than a saw product.

The other actors within this network perceive the tool manufacturers as rather passive in their development activities. One reason for this is that the development activities that have been done by the tool manufacturers have been mainly directed towards improving saws for the mechanical engineering industry. The technical development is summarized in Table 3:2.

Technical development of the saw equipment producers

Investments in real capital have not been of any significance to technical development in other respects. The equipment used is of a standard mechanical equipment type. While the internal mode of operation has been influenced by the development of this type of equipment, the companies have not been affected in respect to other actors.

The day-to-day rationalizations have been mainly a question of successive specialization. The companies have to an increasing degree specialized in a limited range of products. Furthermore,

Table 3:3   Technical Development of the Saw Equipment Producers.

Capital investments:	None that have influenced general development.
Day-to-day rationalizations:	Successive increase in the degree of specialization. Increased cooperation with some suppliers.
Product development:	Many and large. System selling increased. Extensive use of suppliers.

they have cooperated very closely with certain suppliers and customers. This has resulted in new and improved products incorporating electronic, data processing, and hydraulic components.

Thus, product development has been substantial. The features of the products and their degree of automation have in this way been greatly improved. Some examples of new products are: band saws with higher-stretched blades (1969-70) which improved the possibilities for use of the band saw on frozen timber, reductioner band saw (1972) combining the band saw with a reductioner, automatic trimming machines (1973-74), 8-frame (new frame saw 1976-77), and a new generation of circular saw machines (1978-79). Product development has been fast and to a high degree built on new relationships with a limited number of suppliers. The increased use of some new components has also improved the basic features of the product (speed, exactness, etc). In each improvement individual cooperative projects with customers can be identified. There have been rather few contacts with the tool manufacturers. As an example, problems with cracks in the band saws have been solved through developing the band saw machine to parry changes in the tension of the blades with the driving wheel.

Another important product development has been the increased frequency of system selling. The first complete sawing line was sold in 1969. This later became the usual way of doing business until in late 70s when at least some of the larger customers once again took over system design responsibility. In this way system knowledge became important. This was without any doubt very favourable to the largest producer - Kockums. The technical development of the saw equipment producers is summarized in Table 3:3.

Technical development of the saw mills

Sweden was a typical 'frame saw country' at the end of the 1960s. Ten years later, at the beginning of the 80s, there is a whole range of other saw equipment such as band saws, new types of circular saws, reductioners or combinations of such equipment that represents a large part of the production of sawed wood. Thus, there has been important technical development due to investments in real capital. The size of the investments is indicated by the fact that capital intensity increased from 84 000 to 136 000 Swedish crowns per employee between 1972 and 1976. This is dramatic for a group of companies that are known for having equipment with a substantial lifespan.

The saw mills are typical process industries with high costs for raw materials - 60 percent of the turnover. The key issue is the material yield, i.e. the exchange ratio between input (timber) and output (sawed products). In general this ratio varies between 48-52%. A one percent increase means millions of Swedish crowns to the saw mill. Another important issue is the speed of the sawing process, as this determines the production volume.

One important change that occurred in the early 70s was that the saw mills to an increased degree bought complete sawing lines. Earlier they had bought pieces of equipment and assembled them into systems. One reason for this change was most likely that at this point in time several improvements were made to the products. Electronic, hydraulic and computer components were introduced. Thus it became more difficult to assemble the equipment while at the same time the very manner of assemblage became more important. The degree of automization increased which is one indication of the increased links between the different pieces of equipment.

The new equipment was usually the result of intimate cooperation between saw mills and equipment producers. The equipment had been developed and refined during the cooperative projects. This is the case for the reductioner band saw, the computer based trimming machines, pitchsawing with a band saw combined with a reductioner, and the new generation of circular saw machines.

The high degree of capital intensity and the more complicated machines have caused two types of costs to increase consider-

Table 3:4   Technical Development of the Saw Mill.

Capital investments:	Large, new types of sawing equipment have been put in use.
Day-to-day rationalizations:	Successively increased speed and exactness.
Product development:	Marginal and of an incremental type.

ably. These are the costs for breakdowns and maintenance. Therefore both these aspects are today important criteria when evaluating positive and negative effects of different pieces of equipment as well as of alternative ways of buying saw blades. Blade care has also become more important.

The day-to-day rationalizations have regarded production parameters such as speed and exactness. The maintenance problems have as stated above increased in magnitude and have been important problems to solve. Some saw mills have done this by using suppliers in more extensive ways.

Product developments have involved surfaces and exactness in dimensions of the delivered sawed products. There is a common trend towards production of more finished products but these developments have just been initiated. The technical development of the saw mills is summarized in Table 3:4.

The description of the technical development of the saw mill can be exemplified by how a modern saw mill is equipped (this mill is Gruvön in Grums). The mill consists of two saw production lines; one for large-sized and one for small and medium-sized timber. The production line for the large-sized timber consists of two 8-frame saws and two computer controlled trimming machines. The other production line is equipped with one band saw combined with a reductioner, one circular saw combined with a reductioner and two computer based trimming machines. This type of mill where all the different types of saw types have been united is perceived by many experts to be the typical saw mill of the 80s.

Product development within the wood saw network

In this section we will try, firstly, to relate the total technical development process within the wood saw network to the general characteristics of the network in terms of actors, activities and resources. Secondly, and interrelated, we will make attempts to identify the role of product development within the total technical development process.

The wood saw network is very much characterized by the existence of two distinctly different but interrelated transaction chains. Both end in the saw mills. One connects the saw mill with the tool manufacturers which in turn are connected with the steel companies. The other interlinks the saw mills with the equipment producers and their suppliers. The difference between these two transaction chains seems to be of significant importance to the characteristics of the total technical development process as well as to the product development of the various actors. Thus, there are reasons to take a closer look at them.

The transaction chain connecting steel companies, tool manufacturers, and saw mills is featured by repetitivity, standardization and routinization. Furthermore the transformation activities in each step are highly interrelated to the transformation activities in the two others. For example, the transformation activities of the tool manufacturers are highly dependent on the features of the saw steel and vice versa. In the next step the use of the saw blades in the saw mills is highly dependent on the features of the saw blades which in turn are dependent on the features of the saw steel.

This tight activity structure gives the technical development process one very specific feature - its interconnectedness. Development by one actor must be matched by some type of technical reaction by the others in order to be of any use. This favours incremental development steps. There is a continuous process of small incremental technical changes that are all directed to improve transformation or transaction activities.

Even when the changes are incremental there are several difficulties. One problem concerns the variation in preferences between different types of actors. Increased quality features of the saw steel in dimensions giving the saw mills advantages can be difficult to market to the tool manufacturers. The latter are very sensitive to the price of the steel as these costs take such a large share of their total budget (60%). Better steel quality means higher costs and these must be weighted out by increased income in terms of higher prices of the saw blades. But to market higher quality may require more investments in the transaction activities in respect to the saw mills. This is perceived as hazardous by many of the tool manufacturers. Steel companies producing high quality steel have realized this and have instead tried to influence the saw mills - by highly specialized representatives ('saw doctors') - to demand a higher steel quality from the tool manufacturers.

A second type of difficulty is the various ties - technological or others. This can in the wood saw network be illustrated by the development of band saw blades. Usually these blades are used for four houirs by the saw mills and then they are resharpened. It would be meaningless to try to market a band saw blade that could be used for five hours. This is due to the working schedule of the saw mills. Every four hours there is a break and the exchange of the saw blades is done during this break. So, in order to have a marketable product the next level of life length is 8 hours.

Summing up we can conclude that product development within the first transaction chain is characterized by incremental development steps with an aim to increase efficiency in transformation or transaction activities.

The second transaction chain, component suppliers - equipment producers - saw mills, is quite the opposite in nature. Transactions between the units are much more infrequent than in the first chain. Furthermore, there is always an element of unique problem solving in each of them as well as of technical knowledge transfer. In other words there is always a certain degree of technical uncertainty in the transactions and they include several persons (project groups) from both sides. This unique element, however, must not be overemphasized. Productivity demands repetitivity even in these dimensions. This can be attained by the buyers through developing relationships with a few suppliers and by the suppliers by standardization of components or subsystems.

One interesting feature is the change in the borderline between the equipment producers and the saw mills of regarding the division of labour in putting the system together. Earlier, prior to 1970, the saw mills took responsibility for their production system and bought pieces of equipment from the suppliers. Then the equipment producers took over this responsibility in terms of, for example, turn key projects. The trend is now that the responsibility has been taken over by the saw mills (at least the larger ones). These changes are accompanied by changes in the structure of the network. During the period when the equipment producers took over system responsibility most of the contacts with component or subsystems suppliers were held by these companies. Thus, the saw mill worked directly with one supplier who in turn worked with all other suppliers. When the saw mill takes over responsibility of the system design it has to have relationships with a number of suppliers. This causes increased transaction costs for the saw mill but also for the whole network. When the equipment suppliers held these backward relationships the frequency of transaction was higher - they sold several systems per year - which opened up possibilities for repetitivity, learning effects and decreased costs. But again, this gave rise to solutions with elements of standardization which obviusly were seen to be too standardized by the saw mills.

Another feature of the development process within this transaction chain is the use of new suppliers introducing new technology into the network. This process has followed what can be said to be a typical network path. One or a few of the companies with knowledge of the new technology have specialized in applications to the wood saw network, thus successively becoming actors within the network.

A third feature is the importance of social exchange between the actors due to uncertainty in the transactions. To buy equipment or a system is the same as to bind oneself to certain types of transformation activities for a long period. The same equipment can be used for 10 to 20 years. Another uncertainty factor is that the new equipment must work together with the previously purchased equipment and futhermore that it will function under varying circumstances. This uncertainty is especially apparent when the equipment includes new technology. For example, the equipment producer AK Eriksson who is selling band saw equipment, have sold about three quarters of their production to customers within the province where they are located (Småland). The explanation given by the manager was that these local customers knew that they could receive assistance within a few hours if something went wrong. The diffusion of the new technology is in this way influenced by the location of the producer. The occurence of uncertainty has another effect; the importance of reference objects. The potential customer wants to see how the equipment or system functions under normal working conditions. This is one of the reasons why almost all of the new product versions were developed together with a customer. In this way the supplier receives a reference object at once.

In summary, this second transaction chain is predominately characterized by problem solving, adaptation of technical solutions and technology transfer. New technology or new generations of products create interest among the customers, but they also require guarantees in a number of ways. One of the most common ways is by establishing a close relationship with one equipment supplier. Another is to choose the same solution as the other customers. The technical development process within such a transaction chain is featured by both variation and focusation. Firstly, there will be many different types of solutions presented and discussed within the network, but secondly, only a few of these will be used in any large number. The product development of individual actors will follow the same basic structure. One aspect of product development is to develop the actor's principal product, often in an incremental way. Occassionally new technology or new technical principles can create an opportunity to launch a new generation. The latter is important, firstly, in order to convince old as well as new customers that the company is technically advanced and in this way keeping up with the competitors and, secondly, that the basic technological principal can be developed further.

The existence of the two types of transaction chains influence the orientation of the actors. There are many examples of cooperation between actors within the chains but very few between actors in different chains. All the day-to-day contacts are made within the chains and this creates many cooperation possibilities. Still, there is a need for cooperation between the chains. For example, if the circular saw blade is developed this increases the competitiveness of the circular saw equipment producer and vice versa. Despite these possibilities there are few examples of cooperation between equipment producers and tool manufacturers. Instead there is a certain hostility between them. This is also a network question. The situation in which they usually meet is when there has been a breakdown in a saw mill and the question is then who is to blame - the equipment or the saw blade.

The existence of connections between the structure of the activities within the network and the technical development process are obvious from the above discussion. But the latter is influenced by the characteristics of the resources within the network, too. The network relates resources to each other and activates them in this way. There are different types of resources such as raw materials (wood, steel, alloying metals), production facilities, capital, organization (personnel), and knowledge and experience of different kinds joined together by the network. The technical development process alters more or less the combination of these resources and is therefore, dependent on the characteristics of them. All resources do not have the same importance; some are more important or more difficult to change and become in this way more decisive. In the wood saw network there are two resources that seem to be of special importance; the raw material 'wood' and the 'steel production capability'.

Wood is an expensive and scarce raw material which must be utilized in an efficient way. In the saw mills the material yield is about 50% when measured in terms of boards with sharp edges. Thus, about half of the raw material is more or less wasted. Furthermore, wood is not a standardized material, instead it is variable both in internal and external properties[8]. This determines to a certain degree the saw mills' way of acting and judging the equipment and saw blade producers as both of these affect the material yield. From this it follows that important resources of the equipment producers and saw blade manufacturers are their knowledge of and their adaptability to the saw mills. This can to a certain degree be seen in their product development. The saw blade manufacturers have tried to make the blades thinner and increase their software (services) such as maintenance, adjustment, and resharpening of the blades. The equipment producers have developed equipment that (a) increases the value of the waste such as reductioners which produces wood chips that can be sold; (b) decreases the amount of waste, as for example pitch sawing machines and machines with higher precision in sawnotchs.

Another type of adaptation to this characteristic of the resource is that both these types of producers try to handle the saw mills in an individual way.

The second resource playing an important role in the wood saw network is the saw steel production capabilities. There is need of both heavy capital investment and a substantial amount of experience in order to be able to produce the more advanced grades of saw steel. The process type of production makes these actors very sensitive to the scale factor which, in combination with limited and scattered demand, force them to market the product world-wide. This in turn requires standardization. The product development must be focused towards the largest international buyers which in this case has led to a product adapted to customers with high wages.

The effects of technical developments on the wood saw network are rather straightforward and easy to relate to the transaction chains and to the characteristics of the resources. There is, however, a much greater variation that can still be grasped in this type of analysis which will be shown by the next case.

The Metal Drill Network

The conclusions of the wood saw network will be elaborated by comparing it with a network with a similar basic structure. This second network is defined by the function of making holes in metals. First, the actors and the basic structure of the network will be presented. Then the technical development within it will be summarized and then a comparison made with the development characteristics of the wood saw network. The description is made in a much more general way than in the wood saw network, giving just enough information to make it possible to understand the conclusions.

The network

Five main types of actors can be identified within this network[9]. These are the users - mainly the mechanical engineering industry, the producers of the bench drilling machines, the tool producers, distributors selling both tools and machines, and the high-speed steel producers. Each of these will now be described in more detail.

The users are many and varied. The largest users are the automotive and aeroplane industries. In Sweden this includes companies such as Volvo and Saab. But other large engineering companies such as ASEA, Alfa-Laval, Atlas Copco and Sandvik are also large users. The users differ in terms of production technologies as well as in other aspects. Important features of the drilling operation is speed, exactness, surface finish, and noise conditions.

Most of the users buy their equipment and drill tools from distributors. The latter represent about three quarter of the total market for bench drill machines. They are usually local trade companies specializing in selling different types of machines and supplies to the industry.

There are four producers of bench drill machines in Sweden; Arboga Maskiner, Solberga Mekaniska Verkstad, Strands Mekaniska Verkstad, and Widmek. The largest is Arboga Maskiner which furthermore is highly international. More than 70% of this company's turnover is exported. The product manufactured consists of components such as columns, work tables, drill chucks, and power drives. The production equipment is partly standard engineering machines such as lathes, drills, milling cutters, etc. Another major part of the production consists of foundry equipment.

There are only two tool manufacturers: SKF Tools and Wedewågs Bruk. The first of these two is highly international and is believed to be the largest producer in the world of these products while the other is basically oriented towards the Nordic countries. Both of them started to produce drills during the first two decades of the 20 th century; thus, they are well established in this area. Between 60 and 80% of their sales are sold by distributors.

The drills are made of high-speed steel. There were three such producers in Sweden: Fagersta, Uddeholm Tooling and SKF Steel. The last of these started production of high-speed steel during the 1970s, while the two others have a long history. Both of them are among the eight leading high-speed steel producers in the Western Countries, which together represent 50% of the market. The three Swedish producers are highly international and export 80-90% of their production. In order to be competitive these companies need to have a production characterized by

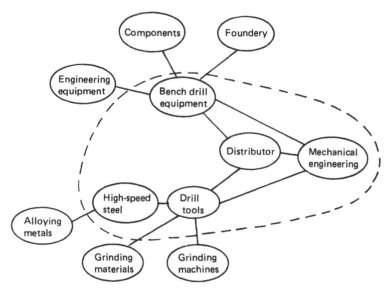

Figure 3:3 The Metal Drill Network.

large batches of the same product. The customers' demands on the steel concern the straightness, the quality of the surface, and high and even internal features. The requirements have increased during the last decade due to the increased production automization of the customers.

The main structure of the network is given in Figure 3:3. The structure of this network is basically very similar to that of the wood saw network. There is one 'equipment chain' and one 'tool chain'.

Technical development within the metal drill network

The major technical developments for the different types of companies, divided into capital investments, day-to-day rationalizations and product developments, are summarized in Table 3:5. Here some additional comments will be made.

The most important capital investments from the network's point of view have been made by the drill manufacturers. The largest of these changed production philosophy in the 60s and then again in the 70s. This has demanded large investments. The other types of companies have also made investments; For example one of the producers of high-speed steel has developed a new

Table 3:5   Technical Development within the Metal Drill Network.

	High-speed steel producers	Drill manufacturers	Bench drill producers	Distributors	End users
Capital invest-ments	Small within strip steel pro-duction. Large in the general production of steel and for one producer a new type of steel.	Large due to changes in production philosophies, first in the 1960s and then during the 70s.	In NC-machines and in com-puterization of pro-duction.	Computer facilities	Increased automatization increased use of multipur-pose machines.
Day-to-day ratio-nali-zations	Substantial, espe-cially in the product mix; specialization of high-speed steel. New production methods have decreased capital investment in storing.	Substantial, especially in production methods.	Important both in production methods and in the product mix. Increased standardiza-tion of components and subsystems.	Large in storing and distribution.	Substantial, varied.
Product develop-ment	Incremental changes are dominant, better internal properties. One of the pro-ducers has launched a new type of steel.	Incremental changes most important. Higher and more even quality. New applications of special uses.	Incremental changes in terms of lowered noise level, increased speed, and increased life length. New multipur-pose ma-chines (pro-duced by specialists).	Increased software — storeless buying etc.	Varied

type of steel which has demanded large investments. This new steel, however, is only used to a limited degree in drill production. A disinvestment has been made by one of the bench drill produc-ers. This company has closed its foundry and instead buys this product from a supplier.

There have been important day-to-day rationalizations in all units. Among the high-speed steel producers there have been important developments within each production step. The con-tent of these has been partly influenced by the need for the steel companies to change their product mix due to the change in production philosophy of the tool manufacturers. Another important change is a new way of organizing production in order to keep the width of the product mix and still reduce the capital invested in stocks.

Among the drill manufacturers there have also been important day-to-day rationalizations. The exchange of production philosophies has opened up large potential for rationalization. There have not been any major changes in the product mixes but some 'exchanges' of products between competitors have occurred.

The producers of bench drill equipment have increased their product mixes. However, due to standardization of components and subsystems this has not resulted in shorter production runs. The rationalization of production has been very important as there has been substantial price press on the product. Product adaptations in order to achieve more efficient production have been of major importance.

Product development has been dominated by successive improvements in the three groups; steel, drill and equipment producers. There have also been some major changes. One of the steel companies has developed a new type of steel, one of the drill manufactures has complemented its product mix with a drill edge grinding machine, and so on. This has, however, merely resulted in a minor change in the total network.

Analysis of the technical development

As in the wood saw network two major transaction chains can be identified. One connects the steel producers, drill manufacturers, distributors, and end-users with each other. The other does the same with bench drill producers, distributors and end-users.

In the first of these two chains there have been two major changes during the last twenty years. During the 1960s there was an increased use in rolling as the main production type of the drill manufacturers. The major advantage with this was cost efficiency when producing large quantities. This type of production was chosen by all the larger producers while some smaller ones, exemplified in the case of the smaller Swedish producer, retained a previous production form. The use of rolling required use of tungsten as one alloying metal; this metal gives the steel the right properties while at the same time it makes the steel possible to roll. However, problems were caused by fluctuations in tungsten prices during the 1970s. Tungsten can be substituted by molybdenum but then the steel cannot be rolled. Instead the production must be built up around grinding operations. The larger producers were once again forced to change their production philosophy. For the largest Swedish producer this took five years. This change was important to the high-speed steel producers, who had to change product mix, which in turn required certain capital investments but mostly rather large day-to-day rationalizations. All these changes had very little effect in relation to the distributors and the end-users. There, the major changes have been related to decreasing total storing without decreasing the total availability of the tools. By increased use of computers and better planning of stocks and transports this task has been fulfilled. The products have been successively improved due to better properties of the steel.

Compared to the same type of transaction chain in the wood saw network there are some interesting differences. The first transaction chain is in general characterized by repetitivity, high interdependence, and routinization, which was also the characteristics of the similar chain in the wood saw network. Still there have been two major changes in this chain compared to none in the wood saw case. These changes have been important to several actors (the producers of alloying metals, the steel mills, and the drill tool manufacturers) and have resulted in new transformation and transaction activities. A condition was that the end-users should not be affected. Thus, there were major changes but within very clear limitations. As soon as the major changes occurred - which took quite a bit of time - all activities were directed towards incremental changes in order to increase the efficiency. The impetus for the change was an uncertainty factor causing extra costs - the price of tungsten. The fluctuation of the price of this product caused severe problems both to the steel producers and to the tool manufacturers. The only possibility to get away from this problem was to change production technology.

Thus, we can conclude that the tight transaction chain is built on a combination of certain resources. If the supply of these resources is changed in some way the transaction chain has to be redesigned. The changes are done in such a way that as few of the actors as possible have to be involved. The changes are done in a 'surgery' form - to change as little as possible and to make the change as local as possible.

The second transaction chain (bench drill equipment producers - distributors - end-users) can be compared to the similar chain in the wood saw network. Some quite interesting differences can be identified. This chain in the wood saw network was characterized by problem solving, uniqueness, and technology transfer. In the drill case the chain features by a rather high degree of standardization. The manufacturers of bench drill equipment have specialized in some types of machines which they attempt to produce in large numbers. Other producers have specialized in multi-purpose machines. One important difference in respect to the wood saw case is that the use of the bench drill machine is much more standardized which in turn is an effect of the characteristics of the material machined in the production operation. In the wood saw operation the material 'wood' varies in several ways and the operation must be adapted as such. In the drill operation the material - the metals - is much more standardized, at least for the main uses. This has made production specialization on an international basis possible. Furthermore the drill operation is, in most of the cases, simply one operation among others. This has caused an increase in the use of combined machines. One of the Swedish manufacturers has developed such a machine but the usual case is that one specialist takes care of each type of product. One end-user described their procedure for purchasing this type of equipment by saying; *We buy the more simple bench drill machines and combined drill and milling cutters from Swedish suppliers, special drill machines are often bought from the U.S.A., and Italian suppliers are normally used when buying multipurpose machines.* Thus, the use of the machines are so similar that the producers can sell them worldwide. But the high degree of internationalization increases competition and requires cost efficient production. This in turn must be met by standardization and large batch production which is best combined with product development in incremental steps.

The comparison of the two cases gives an indication of the complex and multidimensional connections between the technical development process and the characteristics of the network. Here we will limit our main conclusions to the connections between the characteristics of the transaction chain and the product development. These can be summarized as follows.

A tight transaction chain often gives rise to incremental product development, but the changes can be much greater if some basic conditions in terms of used resources are changed. Such change opens up the transaction chain or parts of it and creates opportunities for new technical solutions. As soon as one major solution has been accepted by most of the actors the transaction chain goes back to the tight and closed structure. One important feature of the chosen solution is probably that it should change as little as possible and affect as few actors as possible.

A loose transaction chain creates opportunities for flexibility and problem solving with accompanying openess to new solutions. This is because there are less restricting technical dependencies, as well as other dependencies, within the loose transaction chain. As loose and tight transaction chains normally intersect in certain actors, the former will often be dominated by the latter in terms of product development. The openess of the loose chain is in fact restricted by the influence of the more established 'tight' transaction chain. The product development becomes in these situations open to larger changes in respect to the internal characteristics of the product, as long as the performance of the product from the user's point of view is not changed.

However, a loose transaction chain can also give rise to standardization of solutions (products) which can be sold world-wide. This creates new dependencies in technical, knowledge and administrative/logistic dimensions and tightens the structure in terms of the positions and roles between competing companies. Product development once again takes on an incremental character in respect to the various solutions.

The process of technical development

The process of technical development was at the start of this chapter characterized as a muddling through process combining both political and random factors. It was also suggested that this process takes place within a network featured by

—existence of activity cycles and transaction chains
—instability and imperfection
—specific structure creating limitations.

The two cases have illustrated and supported this theoretical description in several ways. It has been easy to identify activity cycles and transaction chains and also to see their importance for technical development. These phenomena are without doubt important considerations in all technical development.

The instability and imperfection of the networks, as well as how these are used by different actors, can also be seen in the cases. In the wood saw case responsibility for system design shifts, over time, between the saw mills and the equipment producers, as a result of perceived changes in the power distribution. In the same way the drill manufacturers tried to increase their control (power) through an exchange of one raw material for another. The network can in these respects be seen as a social melting-pot continuously confronting different interests. By combining the word 'social' with the technical concept 'melting-pot' we wish to indicate firstly that the results of the process are perceived by the social actors with accompanying variation in judgement, and secondly that most of the power bases are technically oriented in terms of control of resources (raw materials, knowledge, etc) or activities (transformations and/or transactions). Together the social and technical dimensions create the conditions for exchange and thereby for technical development.

The network structure in terms of dependencies between different activities, different resources and different actors, as well as between combinations of all these, allows for little freedom in action. One actor can do very little if the actor is not able to mobilize others in the network. If the actor succeeds in doing the latter almost anything is possible. Thus, the structure is the result of interactions (it is interacted) and must be changed through interactions.

Management Implications

This last section will be devoted to what all this means in relation to the individual company. Earlier in this chapter we discussed some implications in terms of the network as an obstacle to change, as an idea generator, and as an information transmitter. Here the discussion is centered on four issues. The first concerns the question of how generally applicable this type of analysis is; e.g. can it be used in both mature and new technological fields?

The second issue concerns the strategic implications as regards the company. Can the networks be managed? This leads to the third issue which concerns the ability of networking; in what ways can a company improve its ability to survive in a network? The fourth issue concerns one such possibility, namely the company's ability to handle functional interdependence which to a large extent is an organizational problem.

Applicability of the approach

The two cases presented can both be characterized as representing mature technologies. We have however, with encouraging results, used the network approach for analyses of individual as well as groups of companies in relation to their development within other technological fields.

One such field is the marine engine network. This highly international network consists of actors such as separator producers, engine producers, oil companies, shipyards, and shipowners. The analysis regarded the technical collaboration between the separator producer Alfa-Laval, the engine producer Sulzer and the oil company Shell, as well as the accompanying problems of protecting individual product development.[10]

Another study examined the development of a block tool system by Sandvik. The actual network is highly international. One strategic issue for Sandvik was to establish close contacts with some of the producers of lathes without offending others.[11]

A third study examines how a company, one which is well established within one network (the pulp and paper network), tries to establish itself in a consumer product network through product development and later by means of a merger.[12]

The birth of a high-tech network was the object of a fourth study. The network approach proved to be highly useful when describing and analysing the early development of a technological field.[13]

All of the above studies, as well as others which have been conducted, indicate that the network approach is not just a research tool but can also offer useful and stimulating insights for management. Furthermore, the approach is not limited in its application but can be used in quite different areas such as new advanced technologies as well as more established, mature technologies.

Strategic implications

We started this chapter by indicating a certain scepticism about the possibility of managing large companies in a more direct manner.[14] One important reason for this is the existence of networks. The company is interlocked with others - it is not a free and independent unit. Thus, in our perspective management is often involved in wrestling with dependencies in order to create an alternative, in finding a way, rather than of choosing among existing alternatives. The 'muddling through process' can once again be used as a means of identifying important strategical issues. Broadly speaking two issues emerge. The first can be labeled 'get into the mud' and the second 'get through the mud'.

A network must be learnt through working within it. The reaction pattern is namely affected by the entrance of a new-comer, which makes previous in-depth studies of it more or less obsolete. This does not mean that managers should not analyse and think, but only that such activities do not compensate for the necessary experience gained by working within the network. Our recommendation is to learn from what is happening, reflect from all reactions, instead of thinking out and planning everything before hand. It is more important to gain experience than to attempt to do things exactly 'right' from the beginning. The development of a new product can be used as a means to get into a new network, as a way to test the other actors, and to learn how they react. In these situations product development is more of a reconnaissance than a commercial project.

Another interesting effect of membership in the network is that by getting into it, the network will also entrap the new-comer. There will be investments made by the company trying to get in but there will also be investments made by those letting the new-comer in. The larger those investments are the more unwilling the others will be to let the new-comers slide out again[15].

The second issue - to get through the mud - again points to the need for power of endurance. A R&D manager in a successful Swedish company in a speech concluded that:

If I should point out one single most important individual factor for success in product development, I would choose power of endurance without any doubt. It is never the ques-

tion of how good, useful or profitable the idea is from the beginning but how to make it useful and in this way profitable by hard work. Thus, product development without endurance is worth nothing!

The strategic implications are obvious. It is important to have enough resources to force projects through, thus it is better to back up a few projects more heavily than trying to work with several projects. Another implication can be that it is important to find ways to 'mummify' projects instead of completely abandoning them in situations when it is impossible to go any further. The mummifying facilitates a restart when the network has changed in such a way that earlier impossibilities have become possibilities - new materials, equipments, knowledge, etc. The mummifying is in other words a tool for increasing the company's power of endurance.

There are also some other more specific network issues that can be of importance both when getting 'into the mud' as well as when one is working one's way through it. These are the cooperation, the neutrality, and the protection issue. All of these are related to each other which have been exemplified in the cases presented earlier.

Cooperation with others is an important tool both in order to mobilize resources and to use existing resources in a more efficient way. But cooperating with others in product development creates problems in respect to neutrality and protection of in-house knowledge. Working together with one customer can have as an effect that other customers question the neutrality of the company. It is in this way easy to be seen as allied with certain actors. This can have negative consequences and therefore needs to be carefully handled. One way to deal with it is to be open and take part in several different cooperation projects so as to appear neutral in respect to product development. Another way can be to avoid having too clear a policy in these questions. This can be used as an excuse for inconsistencies when dealing with similar customers.

Another related issue is how to protect in-house ideas or knowledge in cooperation projects. The involvement of other companies always implies a certain risk in terms of getting weakened rather than of being strengthened. Although there is no simple solution to this, one important step is to be aware of it. In our case studies we have seen examples where companies have begun cooperation projects but later, when the project moved too close to the unique technical core of one of the companies, this company has taken over the project and continued alone. Another way is to divide the cooperation project; to separate out subprojects which can be completed internally.

Networking ability

Our empirical studies have convinced us that there are substantial differences between companies in their ability to handle the network. Some become highly talented and stable practitioners while others are quite simply 'amateurs'. One aspect of the networking ability concerns the position of the company within the network. The position is defined by the actual combination of resources and activities. Product development means, as we have stated earlier, that these combinations change. In order to strengthen its position the company needs to systematically build further, firstly to improve the integration of its resources and activities, secondly in terms of using its resources in new activities and thirdly by using new resources in the existing activities. These three types of product development are quite different in character from the network point of view. Thus, one critical networking ability is to be sensitive to these differences and organize and judge the different types of resources accordingly.

Another important networking ability regards the handling of individual relationships. Earlier we have given many examples of how relationships can be used in product development. But the opposite can also be important. Product development can be used as a means of showing mutuality in the relationship with an important customer. In this way product development can be utilized in order to secure the selling of other established products.

Functional interdependence

The network approach points out the interdependence between company functions. In this chapter we have covered marketing, purchasing, R&D, production, and economic issues. We have indicated the need to actively use technical factors in marketing and purchasing as well as using suppliers, customers, and other external actors in the company's technical development. This interdependence must be captured by the organization of the company. It can also be formulated as to reflect the network in the organization. In doing this there are two critical aspects which must be considered. Firstly, the organization should not function in such a way so as to underestimate the complexity of the network[16]. It is easy to see the effects on product development if the organization fails in this aspect. Secondly and related, the complexity can easily lead the company to increase the planning and the analysing to such an extent that it more or less replaces activities towards different counterparts. As we have concluded earlier, networks relate activities and actors to each other in such a multifarious way that they require learning by experimental means, thus the company has to 'get into the mud'.

The functional interdependence can be seen in the product development itself. Product development is dependent on a combination of different factors, as shown above, but it also has effects in several dimensions. It can be a means finding new markets but it can as well be a means strengthening established relationships, to show mutuality or power in relation to certain actors, or to increase the interest of, for example, suppliers. It is in other words a genuine network issue.

Notes to Chapter 3

1. Scott (1982 pp 175-77) is as one example critical to both these and we very much support his view. If for example, the change process is looked upon from an investment point of view its seems quite obvious that the speed is decreasing. As the total stock of investments are much larger today new investments even if they are large become more and more marginal. The belief of the need of an active management is very much dependent on an assumption about the possibility of rationality in decision making. This assumption has been criticized by several researchers; for a recent review see Brunsson (1982). Littler (1984) have given the same kind of opinion in regard to product development.

2. This can also be seen in the use of concepts and models as adoption and adoption processes. One explanation to this focusation can be that the economic consequences of a new product usually is of much larger magnitude to the selling company compared to the buying company.

3. This division of technical development into three subgroups is taken from Carlsson *et al* (1979).

4. In every network some main actors can be identified. In our cases they are usually companies or other organizations (e.g. research units). Individuals as actors will be analysed in Chapter 5.

5. An early discussion of cost of change can be found in Carlson (1970). Another related concept is source loyalty - see, for example, Wind (1970) and Cunningham & Kettlewood (1976).

6. This has by others been called unlearning - see Hedberg (1979).

7. Håkansson (1982). The main data collection was done through personal interviews. Twenty technicians and marketers from 13 different companies were interviewed.

8. The wood in different parts of Sweden varies according to this. This type of heterogeneity has earlier been discussed in Johanson & Hägg (eds. 1982).

9. The data collection was done by two students under our supervision - Björk & Edwall (1982). Companies in all categories were interviewed.

10. Kostiainen (1984). This network consists of actors such as separator producers (Alfa-Laval, Mitsubishi, Westfalia and some small producers), engine producers (Sulzer, Buhrmeister & Wein, Mitsubishi and some small companies), oil companies, shipyards, and ship-owners. The need for product development was caused by technical changes in the production of oil products. The network is very well structured and the companies have known each other for many years. Technical development in this case was initiated by Sulzer (the largest engine producer) by a proposal for a cooperation project with Alfa-Laval. The latter responded favorably and furthermore asked SHELL to partake. The product development was one of the results from this cooperation project. One important issue for Alfa-Laval in this case was to balance the need to cooperate in order to get access to necessary resources (for example an engine lab on a ship) with the need to protect the results in order to acquire a patent. Furthermore, working closely together with some partners without being perceived as being joined too closely by other important actors was another objective.

11. Axelsson & Lövgren (1984). Sandvik Coromant is the world leader (25% market share) in the area of cemented carbides for cutting tools. The tools are used in different types of lathes. During the last decades there have been increasing automization which as one consequence has caused an increased interest in the tool holders. The block tool system developed by Sandvik is one attempt to solve this problem in a new way. Development was started in 1976 and very early (after just 2 months) Sandvik tried to establish close contact with four lathe producers; Heyligenstaedt in West Germany, Cincinnati in the USA, Wickman in the UK, and SMT in Sweden. One reason for choosing four was that Sandvik did not want to favour any one lathe producer. In other words, Sandvik did not want to offend any producer. A cooperation agreement for 2 years was signed with all of the above named producers, but the contacts with Cincinnati and Wickman soon died out. In the period 1978-80 Sandvik continued development work but mainly without external contacts. One important exception was ASEA (an end-user) that actively took part in some field tests.

The product was introduced at the Chicago fare in 1980 and that was also the starting point for several minor projects in cooperation with lathe producers as a means of ensuring compatibility. Another group of actors that must be influenced are the end-users (e.g. automotive companies). To change to the block tool system is most interesting for the users when they change the equipment, i.e. make larger investments. In these situations both the lathe producers and the tool system producers are actively influencing the users which can cause triangle dramas.

12. Waluszewski (1985). The study is focusing on technical development in regard to products and production processes in SCA, the largest Swedish producer of pulp and paper. One product development studied regards the introduction of a consumer product which became a commercial failure. Howev-

126

er, the process had opened up contacts with consumer oriented companies using paper as an important raw material. In this way the project led to a merger between SCA and Mölnlycke, the latter being the largest and most powerful of the consumer oriented companies.

13. Lundgren (1985). The automization of image analysis has become of increasing interest partly due to the enormous number of pictures that are produced today by satellites, in hospitals, in the control of processes, etc, but also because of the need of giving robots and other automatic processes an ability to 'see'. In Sweden several research teams, as well as some other organizations and companies, interested in different but related research issues have sucessively, over the last 10 years, built up what can be called an 'automatic image analysis network'. The birth process includes both the creation of new companies such as Context Vision and the involvement of established companies like ASEA (Robotics) and Hasselblad. The new companies have mainly universities or other research centres as their origin. For example, there have been a whole series of companies created around the University of Linköping.

14. See note 1.

15. This type of barriers to exit can in many situations be larger than investments in production facilities. From the individual level it is wellknown for example in relation to gangs of criminals.

16. This can be compared with Weick's (1969, p. 40ff) discussion of organizing as directed toward removing equivocality from the informational environment.

Chapter Four

SUPPLIER MANAGEMENT AND TECHNOLOGICAL DEVELOPMENT

Björn Axelsson

Technological Development and Interaction

The previous chapters have shown that process and product development implies that the individual company's resources, equipment, knowledge, personnel, etc., can be combined with resources which are controlled by other actors in the industrial network. In Chapters 2 and 3 we have seen examples of how this occurs in different types of interaction processes, in various networks, in relation to different companies, in process development as well as in product development.

For the individual company it is a strategically important question to what extent and how it should interact with external actors such as suppliers and customers. A company's total resources are in general small compared to the resources which are controlled in common by the other actors in the network. There is, for this reason, always cause for the individual company to attempt to acquire access to these resources. Practice confirms that some companies choose to work broadly with many suppliers and as such take advantage of a variety of resources and also attempt to avoid dependency on any one supplier. Others select a few with whom they have intensive and often long-term cooperation. A third group chooses not to work together with their suppliers in development issues.[1]

The purpose of this chapter is to discuss and analyze how suppliers may contribute to a focal corporation's competitive power. An important difference between this chapter and the previous ones is that here we are not going to focus on specific product or process developments, but on specific companies' use of suppliers in their development activities.

The discussion builds mainly on the concepts developed in the previous chapters. The strategical perspective, however, calls for an introduction of a number of additional concepts which will be introduced. We shall start with two minor illustrations of companies' supplier management. After that we shall turn to a theoretical discussion in order to elaborate the necessary concepts. The main part of the chapter will be devoted to a special steel study, which is divided into two sections, a case-study section and a key-issue theme section.

Exploiting the Supply Structure - Two Illustrations

The following examples illustrate how two companies utilize their supplier network for technological development. The first company, Ericsson Information Systems (EIS), within the Ericsson group, deals especially with the strategic action of a company which is in the field of advanced technology, namely office automation. They produce office information system products. The other example, Saab-Scania, deals with the way in which a company takes care of and creates development resources in the industrial environment. The company produces lorries, buses and motors as well as gear boxes for automobiles.[2]

Ericsson Information Systems (EIS)

Within EIS there has emerged a concept which sees purchasing and production technology as being important considerations when the product is still in the idea-stage, that is when the company begins specifying new products. One considers the company's future as depending on its ability to create functional supplier networks. This explains why the company not only works with cost-analysis for purchasing versus production but also for purchasing versus development. A decision for purchasing versus production is made from the standpoint of an existing construction. A decision for purchasing versus development is made, on the other hand, from the standpoint of the solution which the customer desires. For this reason, the question is whether such development should be worked out in-house or purchased externally.

The technological development within EIS's field is advancing rapidly. A central ambition for the company is the need to shorten the amount of time needed for development. The point of departure is first off, to exploit those resources which already exist, and secondly, to utilize the suppliers who have competence to develop that which EIS needs. It is important that the vital stages of development can be quickly implemented. Since the company has limited resources, they must to a large extent rely on suppliers. The objective is to learn how to make use of this in an orderly manner.

Saab-Scania

For Saab-Scania the supplier network plays an important role in product and process development. It is vital that the suppliers develop and modify their product according to Scania's needs. The corporation is seen as having various strategically important development suppliers. The company attempts to influence these in the 'right' direction and consciously chooses suppliers according to their development capabilities. The number of strategically important components are a part of the 500 suppliers' articles which represent the dominant expenditures of Saab-Scania. The approximately 250 largest suppliers represent 50% of the corporation's total purchasing, and the strategic development suppliers are highly represented within this group. In a purchasing subdepartment which handles 90 of the 250 suppliers it is estimated that the company has development cooperation with 50 of them.

These illustrations demonstrate a number of reasons for a company's interest in utilizing suppliers in their development activities. The EIS case points to the fact that technological development occurs quickly in many fields and receives impetus from high-tech corporations. The Saab-Scania case stresses the importance of development interactions for a company which uses a large number of components.

In general both production and product technology have become more complex. This is seen in the increased tendency to combine different technologies (mechanical, electronic, chemical, etc.). For an individual company to follow all of these areas, which in different ways are important for the firm, it would be successively forced to escalate its resource allocation for observation and follow-up of various kinds of technological development. By cooperating with suppliers a corporation can increase its possibilities for specialization of its own development. Resources can be concentrated into key areas instead of being spread out. The establishment of development relationships may in other words be a pre-condition for increasing specialization of the in-house development process.

There are, however, a number of problems related to these kinds of actions. There must for example be a certain balance between internal and external development. Some components may be a strategical concern and the development of them should for such reasons be handled internally. The problems with these kinds of relationships also cover such issues as choosing and maintaining individual suppliers, the number of suppliers to co-operate with, developing the cooperation patterns and so forth. From a network perspective the dynamics of the interplay between individual relationships and the company's total relationship structure is a vital concern. For this reason, we shall now discuss the connections between relationships and network positions. Later on five key issuses are going to be identified and discussed.

Relationships and Network Positions

In the production network ongoing activities create change. Some of these activities support others. One example can be when a corporation in the chemical industry have begun to reuse its lubricants and for this reason are faced with corrosion problems. The steel they use may not be sufficiently resistive. The reason for the initial change may be either a political or economic consideration. This activity is most likely followed by new transactions wherein the corporation contacts suppliers of other materials; for example titanium, which is a more corrosion resistant material than the stainless steel which was used earlier. The process of change is effected not only by new supplier activity but also through the activities of the steel suppliers used earlier. These may either limit their activities or else become involved in or increase their ongoing activities in other business partnerships.

The process of change can at the same time also be undermined by forces which seek to support the special steel producers and its customers in relation to each other; that is, to support the production network's existing structure. One example of this is when a chemical corporation begins a dialogue with, or enters into technological development cooperation with one or more of their special steel suppliers. The goal can be to solve the anticipated problems. These anticipated problems can also cause new relationships to be implemented, for example, with other steel suppliers or by the establishing of joint contacts with research centres.

Activities within the production network thus bring together different types of actors and resources and creates relationships of dependency. The interdependence between various relationships in the network implies that a certain corporation's change in behaviour also influences the position of other corporations. It is due to such interdependencies that the interplay between a company's relationships to individual actors and its total relationship structure is of such a vital concern.

This reasoning calls for a distinction between a company's total position and its position in relation to individual suppliers. The total position refers to the production and the geographic networks in which a corporation operates. It also refers to a corporation's strength within certain areas of production and geographic networks. A company can be seen to have a leading or marginal position[3].

The position in relation to individual suppliers refers to the identity of the company's counterparts as well as the amount and quality of the transformation and transaction activities which are carried out with the supplier. The aspects of this kind of position can be viewed in a number of ways; among others, according to the needs and functions the supplier fulfills in relation to the corporation.

The interplay between the individual relationships and the company's total position can have a number of effects. A corporation's relation to a certain supplier may result in product developments and as such contribute to the buyer's total position as for example a technically leading company. The interplay also works the other way around as the buyer's total position may enhance its potential of attracting certain suppliers[4].

The individual suppliers are of varying importance to the corporation due to their contribution to the corporation's actual and desired role in the network. Certain resources are critical. It is for this reason of greater importance for a corporation to gain control over these resources. If the resource is scarce the actors in the network will develop strategies to gain control over what is available. If there is an excess-supply the control of the resource in question is of little importance to the actors. Thus, the importance of certain kinds of suppliers will most probably influence the focal company's activity pattern towards them.[5]

Relationships, positions to individual suppliers, and total position are three important concepts used in the rest of this chapter. In order to achieve an empirical understanding of how certain supplier relationships may contribute to a corporation's position in the network and how this affects the activity patterns, we are now going to turn to our overall theme - a study of special steel usage. With the help of this industrial network we hope to develop a picture of those conditions in which exchange with a certain type of supplier plays a greater or smaller role and how this and the desired interaction patterns change over time.

The Special Steel Study

In the study which is referred to in this section (Axelsson, 1983) 14 important users of special steel have been examined in respect to their utilization of external actors and especially producers of special steel. The study discussed the manner in which the users have utilized suppliers for their own technological development, and how their positions in respect to the special steel suppliers contribute to the users' total position in the network. The study had two main purposes; one was the need to identify and describe how a number of important factors influenced the technical exchange process. The choice of cases was influenced by this purpose. The data was collected from special steel users which were considered as being different in terms of the dominant problems of material, but even referring to differences in the degree of internationalization, the resource strength, the type of industrial network, etc. The objective was to find variations.

The study also attempted to give a picture of how important the Swedish special steel industry was in relation to various customers' technological development. When the examined customers are viewed collectively, the importance of the special steel industry in the industrial network should be indicated. This purpose of the study influenced the selection of firstly, very large corporations with a large usage of steel. The reasoning was such that, through a study of a limited number of cases, we would be able to both capture a perspective picture of the usage of special steel and a large part of the total consumption. In Appendix 2 there is a short description of the Swedish special steel industry's products, those corporations which produce such products, the area of usage for the products, as well as some important Swedish consumers for each product. The 14 selected corporations should be considered in light of this information. Here Volvo, Sweden's largest industrial corporation, is included. Also, the third to the eighth largest corporations are within the sample (ASEA, Saab-Scania, SKF, Sandvik, Alfa-Laval, and Atlas Copco). ESAB, the twelfth largest, and Stal-Laval, the twenty-first, are also included. Kema Nobel, Sweden's second largest chemical concern, along with two relatively small mechanical engineering companies, Sunds Defibrator and Örnsköldsviks Mekaniska Verkstad (ÖMV), are included in the selection[6].

In Appendix 1 seven main groups of special steel products are identified; tool steels, stainless and constructional steels, as well as heavy and thin plates and sheets, tubes and tubular products, cold-rolled strip steel and flat wire, and cold finished bars and wire. Stainless steel and constructional steel are used extensively by the examined corporations. Plates and sheet and tubes are also present in most of these cases. Tool steel is present in only one of the examined cases.

The choice of companies is a compromise between the two goals of the study. The target has been to give a 'representative' picture of the special steel industry's role in the technological development of the production network. At the same time, the aim was to expose isolated pre-conditions for development inter-action. This latter aspect will be given priority in this chapter. The findings which are presented in the following sections are solely based on this study. The idea is to utilize the experience which the 14 cases exhibit.

The study of special steel users has been conducted from a company or group perspective, not from that of individual production units. The interviews have been conducted, first off, within these companies' centrally placed departments for material development. In a corporation's buying centre there are included a number of internal actors, not only those who are purchasers[7]. The most central actors within a corporation's purchasing function there knowing most about material development were considered to be the managers of the material laboratories. These managers have been interviewed according to a systematic interview guide. In certain corporations it was impossible to identify a clearly defined department and in other cases the acting manager of the department did not have an adequate overview of all the aspects we were looking at. In those cases, a greater number of people were, for this reason, interviewed.

The net in focus

The focus of this study is directed towards two types of corporation, namely the 14 examined special steel users and the 8 special steel producers[8]. The study has primarily dealt with the relationships between these two types of corporations. However, these relationships and their importance to a company's position in the industrial network can be difficult to understand if all of the other actors are excluded. The net which is dealt with here becomes for this reason more complex. This is illustrated in Figure 4:1.

Besides the Swedish special steel companies, foreign special steel suppliers which are often the buyer's alternative to a Swedish firm, are distinguished. The presence or lack of foreign alternatives quite naturally affects the relationships, even in relation to technological exchange. Special steel is used in many industrial processes. For this reason the systems of utilization can be comprised of several transaction and transformation structures which are either directly or indirectly dependent on the activities of the special steelworks.

All of the examined corporations, except one, purchase the major part of the special steel they use directly from a special steel company. Some of the companies primarily purchase steel which is further processed in their production (raw material) and some purchase steel which is used in the product as a component. Kema Nobel, a process company, primarily receives the steel via its equipment suppliers. Certain replacement materials are, however, purchased directly. The remaining companies

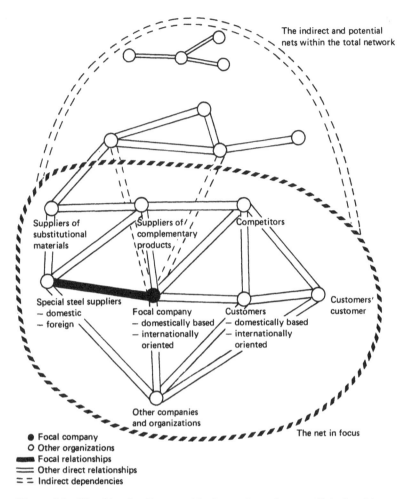

Figure 4:1 The Net in Focus with its various Actors, Relationships and the Total Network.

have their most important steel contacts with the steel suppliers, but for certain steel products they are in practice dependent on several earlier transaction and transformation activities. Examples of this are tools such as drills, which are used in the production of the focal companies' products. These products have normally passed a tool maker who, with material from the steel works, has produced the tool. Sandvik Saws and Tools is the only examined company which focuses on the use of tool steels. This tool maker is directly interacting with special steel suppliers. The user companies from the mechanical engineering industry have consequently direct contact with all of the suppliers but even purchase certain materials indirectly, for example, through tool producers.

Another type of actor in the network is the focal company's competitors. Quite naturally, they also influence the technological exchange between a special steel user and the supplier. A supplier's technological cooperation with a competitor may have both restricting and forward-driving effects on cooperation in the examined relationships. Technological exchange can be considered more interesting if the supplier also works with the company's competitors as this might increase its competence. However, it might also be considered risky due to the possibility of loosing control over critical information.

A fourth type of actor is the supplier of other types of materials which can act as substitutes for special steel. Those who are called other companies are a fifth type of actor in the network. Here is included all other organizations, such as universities, research institutions, consultants, trade associations, etc., with which the corporation has direct contact and which are of importance for the development of materials.

Outside this net is the larger industrial network[9]. In this network we have decided to distinguish two main groups of actors. Certain actors are included in other development nets than those of the focal corporations. Direct contact with these actors does not occur but they can nevertheless influence the focal companies through the interrelated structure of the network. Also separated are potential nets which, like the indirect nets, are not directly and perhaps not even indirectly connected to any one of the examined companies, and for this reason at the present time do not influence it. On the other hand there can exist in these nets interesting developments with potential which in the future can eventually influence the focal companies.

Both the focal companies and the special steel corporations are, as has been seen, connected to each other. The focal company's total position lays the foundation for its competitiveness which is expressed in the corporation's transactions with their customers. The corporation's standing to other separate actors in the network create a more or less sound basis for its total position. The corporation's position depends on the resources which it controls and the value which these resources have for other actors. Relationships to special steel suppliers can accordingly have importance for the company's resource control, its position in the network, and as such to its competitiveness.

Activity patterns and the supplier's importance

For certain corporations the primary value of the special steel producers is their ability to lower in-house production costs, while for other corporations their value lies in the field of product development[10]. Product and process development are two central concerns for discussing and evaluting the suppliers' importance. In some circumstances special steel and the special steel suppliers may be a very critical resource while in other situations they have less importance.

The importance and the circumstances at hand cause the focal corporation to develop separate procedures to handle the various relationships. Some companies work on a selective basis. They select certain suppliers with whom they have a more intensive level of cooperation. Other corporations work on a broad basis. Another difference might be that certain corporations are always involved in development processes; they always have ongoing development activities with steel producers. Again, other corporations initiate development projects on a more sporadic basis. These two dimensions can be used to describe a focal company's activity pattern towards this group of suppliers.

In our study we tried not only to identify the activity patterns and the importance of special steel. Attempts were also made to identify the manner in which the suppliers have contributed to the focal company's competitiveness and also to measure the effects of supplier interaction. The possible indications were judgements such as:

–descriptions of how special steel is utilized by the focal companies and how this affects the user's transactions further on in the production process.
–descriptions of the corporation's technological development over the last 10 to 15 years and in terms of attitudes to judge the special steel industry's importance for the development of the

138

The user's activity pattern	The importance of the special steel suppliers: Very important — The importance primarily related to the Product	Very important — Production	Not very important — The importance primarily related to the Product	Not very important — Production
Selectively/ continually	Alfa-Laval Sandvik Saws and Tools ESAB	SKF	ASEA	
Broadly/ continually		Volvo Car Saab-Scania		Atlas Copco
Selectively/ discontinually	Stal Laval Turbin		Saab Airplane Volvo Aero-engine	
Broadly/ discontinually			Sunds Defibrator	Kema Nobel

Figure 4:2 The Importance of the Special Steel suppliers and the User's Activity Patterns.

focal company. Furthermore a comparison has been made between their importance today and that of 10 to 15 years ago.

Evaluations were also made in relation to how important the domestic special steel industry is, and has been, compared with the influence of foreign companies. Futhermore, the special steel suppliers were evaluated in relation to other material suppliers. The main point has been to relate the importance of a certain kind of supplier to the pattern of interaction with this supplier and to the focal company's total position in the network.

The results are summarized in Figure 4:2. Five of the fourteen investigated corporations work selectively and continually. For three of these companies special steel products are very important to their product and to one it is very important in its production. For one of the five corporations which work selectively and continually, the role which special steel plays is mostly related to the product, but is not very important, (for more details concerning these judgements, see Appendix 1). All these corporations have intensive relationships with certain special steel suppliers.

Three of the other corporations also have ongoing technological exchange with special steel producers but they work on a broader basis. They work broadly and continually. For these companies, the importance of special steel is primarily related to production even though, for one of them it is not judged to be very important. These companies have several development suppliers which they utilize, all of which are on nearly the same activity level. The remaining six of the fourteen corporations work discontinually, among which three selectively choose their partners and two work on a broader basis.

In order to attain better understanding of the dynamics of the activity patterns and the complex interplay between specific relationships and a company's total position we are now going to present two cases, Alfa-Laval and Volvo car, in relative detail.

The main reason for presenting these two cases is to demonstrate the special steel suppliers' role in the focal companies' defense and development of their positions. The organization of the case descriptions is based on Figure 4:1.

The Alfa-Laval case

Alfa-Laval is divided into three business groups; agriculture, industry and the remaining companies. The corporation produces, among other things, separators and heat exchangers for use in the process industry. The case study deals with an international corporation with manufacturing of relatively large series. Special steel is very important for Alfa-Laval's products. Materials development has contributed both to the effectiveness and wider utilization of the heat exchangers and separators. The separators have been used in a number of new ways; always, however, according to known general principles. The most important demands placed on the material are strength in combination with corrosion resistance.

A comparison with the present situation and that of 10-15 years ago shows that much greater demands are placed on the corporation's products at the present time. This means, in relation to separators, that the strength and corrosion resistance of the

140

components are more utilized today. One way of increasing the separator's performance has been to increase the rate of rotation. This has led to increased demands on the material's strength. During the last 10 to 15 years an important increase in both the separators corrosion resistance and strength has been achieved. This development has to a large degree been the result of cooperation between Alfa-Laval and certain special steel suppliers.

In respect to heat exchangers it is primarily corrosion resistance which has been developed. The corporation utilizes the new and improved materials which become available on the market. Development cooperation with special steel suppliers has for these products involved smaller modifications of standard materials.

Relationships with the special steel suppliers

Because stainless steel is the predominant material of concern for the user, the corporation naturally has direct contact with suppliers who produce such material. A substantial proportion of the materials Alfa-Laval buys for production in Sweden comes from domestic steel mills. The corporation buys from the following stainless steel producers: Bofors, Surahammar, Uddeholm, Fagersta and Avesta. The corporation also has contacts with a number of foreign steel mills. When Alfa-Laval was earlier classified as a corporation which operates selectively and continually this was based on the fact that they have more intensive contacts with two of the above named mills: Bofors and Surahammar. These relationships, and the continuous development aspect of them will now be examined.

Alfa-Laval has together with Bofors and Surahammar worked with the development of separator forging since the 1950s. In the beginning either certain types of the so called austenitic steels or the so called martensitic steels were used. Austenitic steel is for most products sufficiently corrosion resistant while strength is not satisfactory. The martensitic steels have good strength but insufficient corrosion resistance. Attention was given, at the end of the 1950s, to the so called ferrit-austenitic steels, which has an interesting combination of the two critical properties. This material was soon produced by Bofors and Surahammar.

The steel proved at first to be very useful. In time, however, a serious weakness of the material was discovered. Severe corrosion was reported when the material was exposed to a chlorine rich environment. Because there was not, in the early 1960s, any available steel on the market which possessed the desired qualities, the management of Alfa-Laval and Bofors started an intensive development project. The metallurgical portion of the project was conducted by Bofors while Alfa-Laval, among other things, developed a corrosion test method which was expected to simulate the practical conditions under which corrosion occurred. This first stage of development did not result in the desired progress. The level of cooperation between these two companies diminished in the following years.

Towards the end of the 1960s the project was reactivated through an initiative taken primarily by the steel mill at Bofors. The project was organized along new lines. A technical solution to the problem was achieved in 1968. When this concept was applied in production, however, such severe technical problems were experienced that the level of cooperation activity, after a time, once again diminished markedly.

Alfa-Laval had also begun a corresponding development project with Surahammar. In this relationship the manufacturing problem was not as great because the latter's production equipment was more suited to this material than the production equipment at Bofors. The level of activity was maintained, and in 1973 a solution was found for the corrosion problem which was even suitable from a production perspective. At this stage another problem emerged. Surahammar is, because of their forgery equipment, a specialist in large forgeries, but Alfa-Laval also wanted to use the new steel in other areas of its product line. As a result of an initiative taken by Alfa-Laval, negotiations were conducted between Surahammar and Bofors which in time led to a transfer of know-how. This exchange resulted in Bofors becoming capable of producing its Alfa-Laval products with the new steel. This material had exceptionally improved corrosion resistance and equally as good strength as the material which was used 15 years earlier.

The development process did not end here. In 1972 Alfa-Laval proposed a cooperation program with the two corporations. The most important demand this time was to improve strength as a means of increasing the separator's performance. Some ten years later this goal was achieved. The project, conducted above all in cooperation with Bofors, time and again encountered new problems; often of a manufacturing-technological nature. The goals achieved, however, have not put an end to the development process. In particular powder metallurgy has in the 1980s opened new and interesting possibilities for further development. Surahammar has developed a powder metallurgical production method which increases forging possibilities and makes new alloy combinations possible. This is the point of departure for the developmental activities which are taking place today between Alfa-Laval and Surahammar. Bofors cooperated as well with Surahammar in relation to their Alfa-Laval product line.

Relationships to domestic versus foreign suppliers

As has been mentioned earlier, Alfa-Laval has relationships with a number of foreign companies. They have also conducted development projects with these corporations. Sometimes development projects are conducted with domestic as well as foreign suppliers at the same time. It is generally understood that the special steel corporations have become of greater importance for the corporation's materials development over the past 10-15 years. This is because external units are generally more important from a development perspective and special steel corporations are the most important actors. The domestic special steel corporations are considered by Alfa-Laval as being somewhat more important than the foreign companies.

Within Alfa-Laval certain differences between cooperation with domestic and foreign suppliers respectively can be identified. Differences in language are an important factor. It is far easier to allocate both supplier and customer personnel within the country. This can often be regarded as a considerable advantage. Communication costs such as travel, translation, etc., are reduced. An important factor is the fact that personnel can communicate easier with others within a specific country. This is because the different personnel share a similar education, as well as a similar way of viewing reality. The most important difference between domestic and foreign communications, according to Alfa-Laval, is the fact that domestic suppliers are usually very interested in their domestic customers. The foreign corporations are much larger than the Swedish; for this reason the relative portion of their capacity which Alfa-Laval utilizes is smaller.

Total position in the network and technological exchange

The description of the separator forgery development is built implicitly upon the corporation's strategy to be a leading corporation within its field. This demands that almost continuous development of the most critical components and most critical materials is carried out. This is also the dominant aim of the project. It is not only the search for new and more advanced materials which causes Alfa-Laval to seek technological exchange with suppliers. Another factor is, for example, the price fluctuations of raw materials. Many stainless steel grades contain realtively high amounts of nickel and molybdenum. Nickel is an expensive metal with great fluctuations in market price. This has caused relatively intensive development activities. A corporation's position is consequently dependent not only on a product's performance but also on its cost.

An important aspect of Alfa-Laval's total position is that it has extensive manufacturing abroad. It manufactures, for example, separators in Italy and Spain. In this respect it is often economically advantageous to purchase materials for such manufacturing locally. It is, for this reason, an important demand from Alfa-Laval that steel which is developed at a specific steel mill can be purchased elsewhere. It is also important that the corporation can use the same steel in the production of separators of various sizes. This latter feature was made possible for Bofors and Surahammar by the fact that they could cooperate with each other.

During the development process with Bofors and Surahammar, a German steel mill began marketing a product with qualities which were similar to those which were in demand. This material was, however, judged to be unacceptable by Alfa-Laval. When they, through their international orientation, received knowledge of the German material, their domestic partners were notified immediately. Later on the German material was improved; for this reason certain foreign steel producers have a product which is very similar to Surahammar's material. This foreign steel was, at a later date, also used by Alfa-Laval. The existence of the German steel has in this case caused the corporation to lessen its demands on the international availability of the developed material. Alfa-Laval has, in their foreign production, been able to utilize the German steel.

The corporation's total position is, in short, very much dependent on its vertical positions in respect to individual actors such as customers and special steel suppliers. Another type of actor of some importance for Alfa-Laval's special steel development is the Institute for Metals Research.

The corporation's position is also strengthened by other suppliers; for example, suppliers of other materials such as rubber. The total position, such as the corporation's international activity and technological advancement influences, in turn, the relationships to the individual actors. An interesting observation is that the dynamics of the network cause a corporation, despite the fact that it can be involved in an intensive development relationship, to nevertheless guard and follow development which occurs in other areas of the network. Despite the involvement with Bofors and Surahammar, Alfa-Laval was conscious at an early stage of the development which had occurred in Germany. The German project was evaluated and as such was an important factor in the decision to go ahead with the project which was underway.

The Volvo Car case

Volvo has a number of business areas wherein automobiles are the largest group. The remaining areas are lorries, buses, heavy and farming machinery, marine, and aero-engines. Thus, the case describes an internationally active corporation which produces in large series. The importance of the special steel suppliers to the development at Volvo lies primarily in the costs of production. The development of special steel has, among other things, caused both lower production costs and also a reduction in the weight of the automobiles.

A comparison of the situation today with that of 10-15 years ago indicates that important development in at least three materials categories has been achieved; they are tempering steels, case-hardening steels and motor car sheet steel[11]. In respect to tempering steels, extensive treatment in the production process demands good machinability of the material. In addition, the material is heat-treated so as to acquire increased strength. Heat-treatment is an expensive process. Volvo's development activities have been conducted according to two lines of reasoning; partly to improve machinability, and partly to make possible the use of less expensive steels. Important advances have been achieved in both of these areas. One example will be described below. Even case-hardening steels, which harden in another manner and partially fulfill other functions, have developed in an equivalent manner. Motor car sheet steel has developed markedly in toughness and strength[12].

Development in all of these areas has to a great extent occurred in different forms of cooperation with individual suppliers. In respect to Volvo this has meant that the corporation has been active and in various ways has joined in development which taken as a whole has occurred in many individual parts of the network.

Relationships to the domestic special steel suppliers

Volvo makes its primary purchases of the following materials from special steel suppliers; bars for forging in its own in-house forge and, finished larger components from external forging shops. Other steel products which are bought from other sources are motor-car sheet steel and special miscellaneous articles (for example, wind-shield wipers). The Swedish suppliers which are utilized are for the most part Bofors and SKF Steel. The corporation purchases a large percentage of their material abroad; in among other places Finland and West Germany. When the corporation was classified earlier as a company which operates broadly and continuously this was dependent upon the fact that they have a number of continuous cooperation projects with various steel producers. Development activities primarily deal with the testing of materials which have emerged from the advancements within the automobile industry, but also within general mechanical engineering industry. In regard to Volvo it is, on the other hand, not common that material development is directed toward individual users' very specific needs. A typical example of Volvo's manner of operation is given below.

Volvo has, since 1973, been involved in a project which attempts to find certain replacement materials for a traditionally hardened tempering steel. When this tempering steel is used to produce certain components, the process is considered to be overly complicated and expensive. The new project attempts to develop a new type of steel which can withstand the demands of performance but which is easier to produce. The innovative aspect is that the steel is alloyed with 0,9% vanadium and that the desired strength is achieved via a different heat-treatment method.

The idea behind the project was introduced in 1973 at a heat-treatment congress in West Germany. The impetus for Volvo was of an economic nature. The material is less expensive, as is the heat-treatment method. One special reason was the need, within a few years, to renew the heat-treating equipment in the in-house forges. The project began in 1974 with a number of Volvo's divisions involved, as well as with a German steel producer. The project then developed in stages. The new steel was tested for its suitability in a specific component by forging a limited number of parts which were then tested. In the event of a positive result a larger number were produced which were tested for strength, as well as for other qualities.

Later the project covered, among others, the following activities.

1974: Test forging in in-house forges of approximately 300 connecting rods type B19. Contacts with SKF Steel and the steel producer at Bofors.

1975: Forging in in-house forges of 40 000 crankshafts type B20 of material from SKF Steel, as well as treatment of such. Furthermore, test forging in in-house forges of connection rod type D20 and D120.

1976: Visit to the German forge wich had experience of vanadium steel. Production of a half year's supply of connecting rod type B21, of this material. Furthermore, test forging of hub and alignment absorbers for diesel motors, as well as test forging of spindles for automobiles.

1977: Decision on materials exchange for hub and alignment absorbers as well as a decision on 100% change-over to vanadium steel for connecting rod type B21. Test forging in in-house forge of connecting rod type D100. Test forging in Germany of spindles for lorries, test forging in England of spindles for lorries. Evaluation in Germany of connecting rod type D120.

In this manner the project continued to branch out. More and more components have been tested and produced using the new material. More and more forges and steelworks have become involved in the work. The new material has, in all types of cutting operations, proved to be more effective, which has been both an important support and an impetus for the project. In one case Volvo has adapted the design in order to make possible the utilization of the new material. An important precondition has been Volvo's accessibility to an in-house forgery for preliminary tests. The special steel suppliers have been broadly utilized: Swedish, German, English, Finnish, etc., have been involved.

Relationships to domestic versus foreign suppliers

Volvo generally considers that special steel corporations comprise an important precondition for the corporation's materials development in the automobile field. The domestic suppliers are considered by Volvo, on the other hand, as not being especially important. The foreign suppliers are, as they have been for the last 10 to 15 years, more important. The most essential differences are that certain foreign producers are more advanced and have greater resources. This can be seen in the transaction activities which occur in interaction with these suppliers.

The Swedish suppliers' representatives often come alone when they visit their customers. As a result they can only be expected to be competent in a limited area of technological expertise. The foreign representatives, on the other hand, often arrive in a large group of experts who operate in close contact with a computer centre, often connected with, among other systems, CAD-CAM capacity. They can, for this reason, make immediate cost analyses of the corporation's components and suggest design improvements. The German suppliers work in the centre of development. Volvo claims that important breakthroughs often come from Germany and that a reason for this is the German suppliers' enormous development capability. They supply many automobile producers and encounter new problems at an early stage and for this reason are always aware of new developments. In respect to Volvo, it is important to be informed and actively involved in the forefront of development which occurs in the corporation's field. Contact is desired with certain suppliers on account of their technological competence. Domestic producers are not as successful because they do not deliver materials to other automobile manufacturers in such large volumes. This limits the importance of development activities with Swedish suppliers.

The geographical proximity of domestic suppliers has little importance to Volvo. The corporation has so many foreign suppliers that those who work in materials must be able to maintain contacts in England, Germany and France as well. To handle these contacts is foremost a personnel and organization question.

Total position in the network and technological exchange

The description of Volvo's development activities is built implicitly on the fact that the corporation's strategy is to be a high quality automobile manufacturer. It is for this reason important to keep abreast and to be actively involved in the new developments which emerge. This should hopefully occur as quickly as possible. The corporation's strategy partially explains the rank ordering of suppliers.

The corporation's manufacturing abroad plays, as it does for Alfa-Laval, an important role in relation to technological exchange. Volvo has a great need for internationally available materials.

Another similarity which Volvo has with Alfa-Laval is the corporation's position in the international network, which means that they often receive information of 'new developments' within the relevant materials area. It is for this reason common that Volvo transfers these ideas and even development projects from these sources to the domestic suppliers. Volvo's primary interest is thus to insure that as many of their suppliers as possible have current know-how.

Volvo's total position is dependent on its relationships with independent actors. The special steel suppliers' primary importance lies in their contribution to production rationality. Other actors which influence materials development are separate research institutes and even other mechanical engineering companies. Volvo has, however, a limited interest in industry joint-research activities.

Both Alfa-Laval and Volvo have shown how relationships and development activities in relation to a certain type of supplier can be handled and in a unique way contribute to the corporation's position in the network. There are both differences and similarities. The relationships with the special steel suppliers are handled by Alfa-Laval in a very selective and continuous manner, while Volvo works broadly and continuously. In respect to Alfa-Laval, special steel is important for the corporation's product while the material's importance for Volvo lies primarily in production improvements. Alfa-Laval sees special steel as a very important resource which has become more important. The domestic suppliers play a central role. In respect to Volvo this group of suppliers is not as centrally important, and the domestic suppliers are less important than the foreign ones.

The two corporations have in common the fact that their total position in the network, their international activities and technological know-how, influence their development activities. The need for internationally accessible materials is shared by both corporations as is the need to retain technological prominence.

Relationships and Positions - Five Themes

The two cases illustrate the complex and dynamic nature of the technological development on industrial markets. They also illustrate a number of key issues to be dealt with; some are outspoken and some are not. In this section we shall widen the perspectives somewhat and utilize the experiences which have been gained in all the 14 cases of the study. Five themes, all of which in unique ways influence the corporation's relationships and positions in the network, will be identified. In the identification process Figure 4:1 has, as in the structuring of the Alfa-Laval and Volvo cases, been a useful tool.

The first issue concerns the focal company's efforts to encourage suppliers to conduct technological development in a manner which is advantageous to the buyer. A focal company not always chooses but at times also becomes chosen by its supplier. An important issue is how a company reaches and maintains a desired position in respect to a certain supplier. A specific aspect which is going to be the focus of the first theme is how a company by various means strives to control its suppliers and the resulting problems.

A second issue which is closely related to the first one concerning choice and control of suppliers concerns the observation of technological areas which for the present are not important for the company but which may be of interest in the future. This is a specific aspect of the choice and as such focuses the time-perspective. It will be regarded as a matter of balancing weak and strong ties (Granovetter 1973). In order to take advantage of certain suppliers' resources there is a need for intensive contacts, and in order to follow new developments outside these relationships there may be a need for a number of less intensive relationships.

The first two issues deal primarily with choosing and maintaining suppliers. How this takes shape in the specific case most likely depends on a number of factors. The next three issues all deal with explanatory factors.

The fundamental conditions which are required for cooperative relationships is that the parties complement each other. From the purchasing company's perspective the supplier should be able to contribute to the desired development. A specific aspect which may influence the choice is the geographical and psychic distance between the actors. It is for many companies more difficult to undertake development activities at long distances. How the distance may explain the development activities is going to be elaborated in the third theme.

The properties of the focal company, i.e. its resources, production technology and its organization, influence both its needs and possibilities of cooperation. A specific aspect which is going to be dealt with in our fourth issue is the importance of the company's organizational structure, specifically its degree of internationalization. Obviously there is a connection between this aspect and the previous ones concerning the importance of the distance between the actors.

The fifth issue that is going to be dealt with is the influence of the industrial network in which the company operates. In the Alfa-Laval and Volvo cases the importance of a number of net-work properties are indicated. This is also true for our introductory illustrations, Saab-Scania and Ericsson Information Systems. The high rate of technological development within EIS's field of production in combination with the company's relatively limited development resources causes extroverted behaviour on the part of the company. Of course, there are also a number of other dimensions of the network which influence development activities, not least the number of available suppliers. Such aspects are to some extent going to be elaborated in the fifth theme.

Supplier control and technological development

For some of the 14 examined corporations, special steel is a very important resource. An important objective for these corporations is to, in individual ways, attempt to gain control of special steel resources. This control can be direct via ownership or indirect via other forms of ties. An important basis for exercising indirect control over an actor is to control resources which are important to them[13].

This understanding is expressed by Stal-Laval Turbin as such;

> *In respect to Stal-Laval it is important to be able to utilize the suppliers' resources in cooperative relationships. This understandably demands that Stal-Laval also has resources which are of interest to the suppliers since they would otherwise receive nothing in return.*

Often a number of transaction activities are also needed so that those resources the user controls can be made available. In relation to Stal-Laval this means that at times the corporation must in a very active manner market their development needs. The suppliers sometimes claim that Stal-Laval wants to achieve properties which are impossible to attain, for example, toughness and high heat resistance. The corporation has sometimes begun its own laboratory experiments. When Stal-Laval could prove that the desired results were possible to achieve in the laboratory they have once again approached the suppliers. It sometimes occurs then that the suppliers are motivated into mobilizing their resources. Through in-house laboratory tests Stal-Laval has at times nearly forced certain suppliers into development activities.

Ownership of resources, and activities for mobilizing and developing resources are consequently important. This is made easier if the corporation controls the actual resources. An important distinction can be made between those corporations which attempt to gain control of special steel directly respective indirectly. Both Alfa-Laval and Volvo can in principle be said to work

152

with indirect control[14]. This means that they attempt to create liaisons through relationships, such as technological, social, economical, etc., with the suppliers. This is the dominant manner utilized by the examined corporations. There are, however, three corporations which have direct control in the form of ownership of a special steel mill. These are Sandvik Saws and Tools, SKF and ASEA. This legal connection strongly affects the corporation's relationships. In respect to ASEA and SKF, this means that the special steel division has a special position and is always given priority in the corporation's development activities. This also applies to Sandvik Saws and Tools, which has very intense contacts with their 'own' mill. They have, among other things, a formal cooperation team in the steel mill's research department. Spokesmen for both sections meet regulary and review current questions. The dominant portion of the tonnage is purchased from this internal supplier. Materials which cannot be supplied internally, (among other things, high-speed steel for metal saws), causes, quite naturally contacts to be made with external suppliers. All three corporations have, most likely, great power over their internal special steel suppliers, which not unreasonaby are also utilized in development concerns.

It is, however, interesting to note that Sandvik Saws and Tools has in the past few years established contact with an external supplier as a complement to their internal supplier. An important reason for this is that this is seen as a means of observing the competitors. The corporation meets, in a larger perspective, a relatively large group of competitors from, among other countries, the USA, West Germany and England. Observation of these corporations is made easier if the company for certain special steel products can utilize the same supplier, especially since the material for this kind of user is of great importance for the product's performance. Through supplier contact the corporation receives worthwhile information about their competitors. These alternative suppliers have consequently an information function for Sandvik Saws and Tools, which is dependent on this information.   •

This line of reasoning means that the value of controlling a supplier through ownership, is not only dependent on the supplier's direct resource control, but also on its other relationships and its total position in the network. Ownership and direct control of a special steel supplier does not accordingly always solve the resource problem - at least not if the controlled corporation does not have a position as a leading technological company.[15]

The special steel supplier's resources and total position in the network consequently have great importance for the value of the user to control the supplier. This is structurually an obvious conclusion of the discussion. There are, quite naturally, even dynamic aspects of this.

To the user, it is important to observe and develop, or conform to the resource structure of the suppliers. Saab Aeroplanes, for example, demanded better than standard quality of a certain material. After using the standard material it was found, with the help of newly developed measuring techniques, just what the new demand should be. Still, they were unable to interest any of the suppliers. The corporation continued to work with the imperfect standard material. Meanwhile, the ongoing development in the network, especially with the established suppliers, was observed. When one of these, for other reasons, obtained a vacuum-remelting furnace, this event was evaluated at Saab Aeroplanes. It was found that this new investment made by the supplier should make it possible to seriously increase the demand for the material in question. This was then the first step in development cooperation which resulted in a considerable improvement. The supplier's new equipment was the decisive condition for this cooperation, but it was also important that the customer actively and attentively followed the suppliers development. Through this observation, Saab Aeroplanes was able to mobilize the supplier's resources in a cooperative exchange which strengthened its own position. In this case even the supplier was able to strengthen its position as a result of the exchange. The development project built up the supplier's competence and made possible more advanced problem solving. An effect of this was that the special steel producer later was established as the supplier to a number of new customers who place high demands on the product.

The special steel suppliers can also change their total position through their own efforts or as a result of changes in or outside the network. ESAB is a company which has experienced the effects of such a change. ESAB has worked with indirect control in its attempt to gain availability to the resources of the special steel suppliers. The corporation has business exchanges with several domestic and foreign special steel producers. It is, however, mainly with one domestic producer that they have had intensive contacts. The relationship has influenced both partners' operations. This can be seen, in among other ways, by the fact that certain categories of new employees at the steel mill have begun their term of employment by working a few weeks at ESAB. The idea has been to help employees become aware of the customer's technological problems.

The special steel producer in question is one of the world's leading manufacturers of stainless steel welding wire. It delivers materials to ESAB's factories in Sweden and abroad as well as to ESAB's competitors. The supplier has also, for certain of ESAB's less important business areas, sold directly to the final users through its own subsidiaries. In these cases it has been in direct competition with ESAB, without jeopardizing the relationship.

During the last years, however, the steel mill has decided to develop its position. This was done through a widening of the welding program so that it included their own direct sales as well as sales of other companies' products. The result of this was that ESAB's traditional partner had now become a serious competitor in ESAB's field of specialty as well. The atmosphere between the partners changed radically. ESAB has suffered diminished accessibility to an important resource and at the same time felt its total position seriously to be threatened. A special reason for this was that the steel mill had been able to learn from those experiences which the earlier cooperation with the user ESAB had given. In this case, most likely, the possibility of such a dramatic position deterioration would not have been possible if the user had had effective control of the supplier.

All these examples illustrate the dynamics of power and the importance of evaluating the supplier's position. This should not only be done at a specific point in time. Also, continuous follow-up and observation is needed.

One conclusion of this discussion is that the dynamics and varying qualities of the industrial network make necessary the need for a corporation, regardless of whether or not it controls its resources directly or indirectly, to actively follow and guard the network's development. This regards both the network as a whole and the individual actor's position and resource changes. An important aspect of this observation in turn is that there in general exists a time factor in regard to a corporation's control over another corporation. It takes time and a certain amount of resources for a corporation to modify its control of another company. The more sensitive these time factors are the easier it is to alter control of the actor. Kutscher (1982, p. 375) uses the term 'time elasticity' to define this phenomenon. Because the dependency of the supplier is related to the user's control, another conclusion is that the higher the time elasticity, the more flexible the time factor is in relation to this dependency, the quicker the user can lose control. A greater time elasticity demands, for this reason, more intensive observation of the network and greater preparedness to conduct suitable activities in order to defend and develop the position.

The discussion in the entirety of this section proves the need, in the operation and development of resource control, to not only focus on the relationship with a certain supplier and the current exchange with him, but at the same time to survey the whole network. This is so even if the supplier is a critical resource. Dyadic relationships are embedded in a wider network of relationships. For this reason at least portions of the remaining network must be included. Analysis and evaluation of an isolated actor's power and resource control in an industrial network demands, for this reason, a multilateral analysis[16].

Choice of suppliers and new developments

Individual relationships are only links in a chain. In order to put the corporation into focus we have made a distinction between the direct network with which they have their own direct contacts, and the indirect network, which can utilize the same resources but where the corporation has only indirect contact through the relationships of dependency in the network. Such indirect networks did not have any prominent importance for development of special steel in respect to Alfa-Laval and Volvo. There are, however, such examples among the remaining examined corporations. We shall discuss here three such examples. The first of these is Stal-Laval.

The point of departure for Stal-Laval's development activities

156

in respect to materials is normally that the materials producer and the aero-engine motor producers, in this case an indirect network as regards Stal-Laval, develop temperature tolerances to a certain level for circa 5 000 operational hours. A difference between an aircraft motor and a stationary turbine is that the aircraft motor usually operates during a relatively short period. In a stationary gas turbine the components operate for approximately 100 000 hours. The producers of stationary turbines must consequently begin where aircraft motor producers leave off and develop components which live up to these demands. In respect to this problem they are pioneers. Another section where the corporation is a pioneer is in developing the size of the components, which are much larger than those in aircraft engines. This up-scaling can be very problematic.

Generally, there is a relatively limited interest, on the part of the materials producers, to satisfy Stal-Laval's needs. This is partly because stationary turbines is a more limited market than aircraft motors, and partly because Stal-Laval is a small corporation. Stal-Laval manufactures approximately 12 gas turbines each year while the aircraft engines producers each manufacture hundreds of jet motors every year. There is competition, consequently, for utilization of the materials producer's resources. The corporation is forced at times, as has been shown, to conduct very active marketing in their contacts with the suppliers. Despite the fact that the 'aviation network' is so important for Stal-Laval, they have limited direct contacts with the aviation industry.

The fact that development activities in a network are the permanent foundation for development activities in another network is interesting but not unique to Stal-Laval. Our second example is Atlas Copco.

The basis for Atlas Copco's development can be found in the 'automobile network'. The automobile industry exerts a great deal of pressure on the materials producers. Overall, they are very large customers for the special steel suppliers; for this reason the automobile industry is well received when they demand product improvements and resource mobilization. The automobile manufacturers are, in addition to this, often more competent in evaluating the material's qualities. Atlas Copco has, for quite some time, been able to take advantage of the

157

automobile network's development because the corporation utilizes the same resources. Atlas Copco has been able, in cooperation with suppliers, to make smaller adaptations of the materials which others have developed in respect to their own specific needs. The material's importance for Atlas Copco has meant that the corporation can primarily be satisfied with observing the material's development which occurs in the automobile network.

An effect of the dependency on this indirect network is that Atlas Copco, to a significantly larger degree than the automobile producers, must be involved in the cooperative research programmes pursued by associations such as Jernkontoret (The Ironmasters Association) and Mekanförbundet (The Trade Association of Mechanical and Electrial Engineering Industry). This is also seen in the fact that the corporation's manager of the materials laboratory at the time of the study was the chairman of one of the latter organization's research committees. In this way Atlas Copco receives information and insight of the broader research going on in the field. Atlas Copco values this cooperative research relatively highly, as does Stal-Laval. An important difference between Stal-Laval and Atlas Copco is that special steel is very important for Stal's competitive power, while it is of less importance for Atlas Copco. This, naturally means, that it is relatively more important for Stal-Laval to gain control of this resource. This explains, most likely why Stal-Laval works selectively while Atlas Copco works with a large number of suppliers.

There are also certain variations on this theme. Not only indirect but even potential nets can temporarily influence an individual actor or an entire net. Of course, a new net can also be an established section of an older one. An example of this occurs in electronics, which has become established in a number of nets.

Sandvik Saws and Tools is our third example. It is an interesting example of how activities in a potential network influences the corporation's development activities. The corporation considers that certain actors which are not included in the corporation's established development network possess very interesting resources in the form of facilities and knowledge. These could, if the resources were mobilized in Sandvik Saws and Tools' favour, be very worthwhile for the corporation's development. There have been several attempts to interest some of these actors but these attempts have not succeeded. A possible reason is that they are already involved in the competitors' development network.

These examples clearly illustrate that for many corporations it is important not only to observe the development which occurs within the company's own etablished network, but also follow development in various indirect and potential networks. Many of the examined corporations have, created organizational bodies which, among other things, have the task of contributing to these ends. Sandvik Saws and Tools has, for example, their own research center in the United States. Through this laboratory the corporation is directly involved in current research activities. SKF has a research center in The Netherlands which was purposefully located in central Europe as a way of easing the recruitment of international researchers. Many corporations also utilize international consultants with whom they maintain ongoing contact. ASEA for example, claims that the most important external resources in respect to materials development are a number of such contacts which are included in its scientific advisory board. In conjunction with these members an extensive review of new technological development is conducted a number of times each year.

One conclusion of this section is that the choice of suppliers and the modes of cooperation must not be static. Influences both within and outside the focused net cause modifications of the supplier network and the cooperation patterns. The examples clearly illustrate the importance of having a number of weak ties to follow the development and make actions possible, and at the same time to have a number of intensive relationships in which joint development activities take place.

Distance and choice of suppliers

Transaction activities act to overcome the gap between actors in the network. The gap can be caused by a number of factors and can be measured in several ways. We can, for example, distinguish between 'hard' dimensions such as the physical or geographical distance between actors, and 'soft' dimensions which are related to attitudes and values which are caused by, for example, differences in cultural environment in a broad perspective.

The soft sections of the gap are of special importance in

159

international transactions because differences in cultural concerns are more prominent in these situations. It is also likely to be of unique importance when the transaction activities are characterized by technological exchange. For example, in Håkansson (1979), it is seen that the Swedish special steel producers' relationships with domestic customers are markedly different from their relationships with foreign corporations. There are, among other things, a larger number of people who are actively involved in the domestic relations, as well as a broader technological exchange. In the Alfa-Laval case, it was seen that the relationships with domestic suppliers played an important role. Most importantly, certain of the soft dimensions, such as language and cultural similarities, were given prominence. This was seen to be the case, despite the fact that the corporation is highly internationalized. In respect to Volvo, this was not considered to be a problem. In both cases this was a cross-section evaluation made at the time when the survey was being conducted. The evaluations indicate that the distance, in a broad perspective, between actors, is an important factor as a means of understanding the development process.

In this section we shall, using information available on the 14 corporations presented earlier, discuss certain aspects of this distance; not however, as a cross section but through comparisons between the situation of today and that of 15 years ago.

Looking back over time, five of the 14 users consider that the Swedish special steel corporations have become somewhat less or much less important for their development. Five consider the special steel mills' importance to be unchanged and three consider their influence to have increased somewhat. An important difference between these various groups of users is that when the domestic corporation's importance develops positively, the suppliers and users support each others' development. They move in the same direction. The resources which the special steel suppliers procure and develop - partly as a result of transactions with these users - agree with the users' needs and demands.

Within the product field for stainless steel, Alfa-Laval, Sunds Defibrator, ÖMV and Kema Nobel are examples of user corporations whose development to a large extent matches and is matched by the Swedish special steel industry. The development of Alfa-Laval's separator forge, which was described above, illustrates a process where the actors' resources are complementary and are applied step by step in developing the product. It is clear that the process itself is very important. The gathering of information and the successive agreements which take place demand that the actors change and develop in a matching manner. This adaptation is multidimensional and includes, besides technological resources, even social and organizational aspects. The complexity of this is indicated by Alfa-Laval's experiences in other situations when they have changed development partners. They have, in a number of cases, attempted to transfer development from one supplier to another with apparently equal facilities. This has, however, often not succeeded because of the multidimensional heterogeneity.

In those cases where the Swedish special steel corporations' importance has decreased, an important reason is that the actors develop in separate directions. They develop, both by themselves and in cooperation with other actors, resources which are becoming less and less complementary. Their activity cycles diverge. Examples of such relationships can also be found in the stainless steel group. In the special steel study we have at least three prominent examples of this phenomenon.

Stal-Laval is our first example. The company has, because of the varying sizes of stationary and marine turbines, been in need of larger forgings than the Swedish mills can provide. The steel mills have not kept abreast of Stal-Laval's development; instead they have concentrated on other areas such as other steel products, as well as other types of industrial activities. The user who meets this development finds it natural to search for and when in need intensify cooperation with other partners, that is to say, with other domestic or foreign suppliers.

Atlas Copco is a corporation which at present is actively moving away from the Swedish special steel producers. The corporation is in need of steel which has an average quality rating. Despite this fact, they have for a long time used products from the Swedish special steel producers. One reason why they are now abandoning these suppliers is because the suppliers to a greater extent limit themselves to producing special steel grades and are less interested in the more simple materials. This means that Atlas Copco is forced to purchase material of a higher quality and price than is necessary. The corporation is now searching abroad for sources of cheaper grades which the domestic suppliers no longer wish to produce.

Even Volvo Aero-Engines, which is our third example, has encountered this phenomenon by experiencing diverging activity cycles in relation to the special steel mills. One difference is, however, that other materials have been substituted for special steel. In the aero-engines, which the corporation produces, the amount of special steel which is used today is approximately 20% (of volume), while in 1950s it was approximately 80%. The critical material for this manufacturing is at present super alloy. The most important suppliers are foreign materials producers.

The three descriptions give the impression that a break or reduction of business exchanges between certain suppliers and users normally does not depend on the fact that the relationships are broken as a result of disagreement over contract terms, but depends instead on the fact that actors develop in different directions. A major finding in the study is that in those cases when there exists one or more domestic producers, that is to say, in those cases where the respective user and some domestic corporations' development match each other, the steel mill is normally utilized in the user's technological development.

On a broader network level these divergent activity cycles are probably becoming more and more common as a result of the industry's specialization. Through specialization the individual supplier is responsible for an increasingly limited product line which is marketed within a large geographical area. The individual user is responsible for a smaller part of the product line. These tendencies probably lead to increased importance of technological exchange with external actors for the users, regardless of their standing in the production system. Support for this argument is found in the fact that almost all of the examined corporations consider development cooperation with external actors as becoming more and more important. The tendency means, at the same time, that a certain supplier is compatible with fewer users within a given geographical area, (for example, a country). The tendency towards specialization, in relation to this argument, has also generally made it more important to possess the capability of conducting developmental cooperation in an international environment. A probable effect is also that the Swedish special steel mills in an increasing tempo will seek to conduct developmental cooperation with foreign special steel users.

The physical and psychogical distance between actors plays an important role in technological exchange. The distance, in many cases, can be an obstacle for technological cooperation, as is also the resultant specialization and internationalization tendencies which become more and more important to overcome.

Activity patterns and production structure

The corporation's level of internationalization varies in a number of ways. The corporation can, for example, be based completely on the home market, as is the case when all of the production and sales is conducted within the country. For many corporations, an initial step into the internationalization process is through direct export. The second step is via production abroad, which can be organized in a number of ways (see Johanson & Wiedersheim-Paul, 1975). Some corporations conduct a global strategy and have an international production specialization. The user's activities, in various geographical networks, especially its own production abroad, influences the relationships with special steel suppliers. The user's international activity creates as such both obstacles and limitations, as well as possibilities for technological exchange.

In respect to Alfa-Laval and Volvo it was found that the importance of internationally available materials was a result of the corporation's international production. There is no equivalent to this in respect to the home-market based corporations. This is the case, despite the fact that all of the examined corporations have a large volume of export trade. The importance of the material for the user did not seem to be influenced by the international factor. Even, for example, Stal-Laval, whose products are very important for the user's transformation activities, the demand on international material is not especially prominent. Demands on internationally available materials are operative, on the other hand, at Saab-Scania and ESAB, both of which conduct production abroad. Within ESAB this means that new electrodes which are developed must be specifically described. An electrode has a certain identification number and is used throughout the entire company. There is a product committee which organizes product development.

163

SKF and Atlas Copco also conduct production in many countries. They avoid, however, this pattern. For these corporations the demand for internationally available materials is not as great. An explanation for this is probably that they have divided up production within the company. These are examples of companies with a globally organized production. In respect to SKF this means that a certain type of bearing can be produced in Italy, another type in Germany, a third in Sweden, etc.. By way of such specialization there is a noticeable lesser need for internationally available materials, which in turn increases the possibilities for 'specialities' in their materials.

These examples have, for the most part, dealt with obstacles and limitations which are caused by the user's international activities. These obstacles can, depending on the corporation's organization, be more or less bothersome. The obstacles are frequently due to the need for internationally available materials for those companies who have an international production structure. The importance of this was, however, due to the specific manner in which the production was organized.

The user's international activities can also improve the possibilities för technological exchange. This was shown in both the Alfa-Laval and Volvo cases. An important feature is thus that the user can 'take home' ideas and sometimes even development projects. The network operates in this case as a source of information.

Activity patterns and network characteristics

The themes discussed above have, in various ways, demonstrated the dynamics and complexities of various networks. The point of departure has been to illuminate the manner in which various characteristics of the relationships and of the users influences their activities and positions in the network. In this section the network characteristics will act as the point of departure.

A network can be characterized in a number of ways, among others, the level of structuralization, the level of concentration, the density, and the variability (Rogers & Kincaid, 1981). In a tightly structured network the actors have well defined roles which are well known to all. The preconditions for technological development in such a network differ from those in loosely structured network. In a tightly structured network the development must, for example, be compatible with the network's development in order to succeed. If it is compatible there might quickly occur demand of new developments.

The special steel industry is in general a tightly structured network. This is not surprising due to the fact that we are dealing with a mature industry. On the contrary, the examined corporations are embedded in a variety of nets and they are all related to the special steel net in various ways. There exists a number of interesting aspects of how the tightly structured special steel network influences the examined corporations' activity patterns.

In Volvo's case, it was shown how the corporation highly values certain West German suppliers. An important reason for this is that these supply a large number of automobile manufacturers and for this reason find themselves in a centre of development. Volvo, a corporation which attempts to maintain a position as a high quality producer must, for this reason, conduct relatively intensive relationships with these suppliers. This network is heavily structured and the technological development is concentrated in certain key areas. Such is the case in West Germany. Volvo is not by itself such a centre. In order to attain development resources it has to try to join this centre. An interpretation of Volvo's behaviour is that a corporation which is not the center of a certain development but seeks to maintain and develop its position in a well structured and highly concentrated network, must have relationships with at least some of these key areas.

Tightly structured and highly concentrated networks can also be expected to influence the corporation's pattern of activities in relation to change. The Stal-Laval case illustrates this phenomenon.

Some years ago both aircraft motor manufacturing as well as stationary gas turbine production had as a goal to produce an alloy which could be used at higher temperatures, and additionally, with better strength. A number of alloys were developed by the individual suppliers. It is not possible at this time to suggest that any of these alloys were the best. But because one of the more prominent users decided to use a given alloy, the ice was broken. All of the others sooner or later also began to use the same alloy. The other alloys which were probably comparable were never used. Such an activity pattern, which not only has a 'follow the leader' aspect but also a 'snow ball' effect is probably very common in the tightly structured networks. Furthermore the more the chosen alloy was used, the more experience and test results were accumulated, the less reason there was to utilize other alloys of which little was known.

It can be a direct coincidence that someone took this first step. It demands a certain experimental daring, but the choice is to a large extent random. There remains a number of unproven possibilities. The corporations have invested in one direction and see no reason to work in others. If this is to occur, there must exist, for example, a shortage of this alloy, or desire to additionally increase the temperature tolerances by a number of degrees. Under such conditions other alloys would once again become interesting.

An interpretation of this is that when the heterogeneity and uncertainty of a resource is great the development is characterized by caution. For this reason experience plays an important role. The network brings about, in various ways, a pressure to adopt that which works well. The network makes it visible. These types of network effects are likely to be most prominent in tightly structured networks where the actors' roles in the network are clear and well known to all.

Concluding Remarks

The chapter began with two examples of how a corporation considers and works with their suppliers in developmental matters. A conclusion of this was that a corporation can strengthen and develop its positions in the network through various activities as a means of utilizing and controlling resources. The conditions for this were scrutinized with a study of the special steel industry as the point of departure. Special interest has been devoted to the interplay between single relationships and the network.

There are many lessons to learn from this chapter. Here only three aspects will be dealt with. These are the need for strategic consiousness of the importance of external resources, the need to act and react in the network as well as the need to control resources.

The need for strategic consciousness

There are many reasons for a purchasing corporation to become involved in developmental work together with its suppliers. Compared with a total non-involvment in these questions, the interaction of the purchasing corporation creates possibilities for guiding and controlling the suppliers' developmental processes. This interaction also means that the corporation receives accessibility to and can utilize resources which they themselves have no ownership of. The acceptable level of external relative to internal development becomes a question of weighting the possibilities of controlling others as against the availability of the development resources.

Another very important motive for cooperation is that it means that development in the purchasing corporation is more easily placed in harmony and coordinated with development in the supplier corporation. The network operates as an obstacle to technological development while at the same time creating opportunities for it (see Chapter 3). In certain networks great demands are placed on the new development to fit into the network structure. Through interaction the purchasing cooperation is guaranteed that its own development is in line with the network's development. This is also a way to utilize the suppliers' development activities to a greater degree, seeing as they can be designed according to the purchasing company's needs. There exists, quite naturally, risks with development cooperation because changes within an indirect or potential network in the long run can beat out the network which the corporation for the present is a member of. This causes the corporation to also have a need to observe the various networks' development in relation to each other. Despite a high level of involvement in a number of supplier relationships, the corporation must accordingly be able to create and maintain possibilities for new combinations.

In order for a corporation to best be able to utilize those opportunities which exist in cooperation with the suppliers, a conscious understanding, strategic awareness, as well as an understanding of the opportunities and limitations which such cooperation includes are all necessary. This strategic awareness should act as the starting point for evaluation of internal versus external development; which materials, components, facilities, etc., should be developed internally rather than externally, as well as the choice of the individual suppliers. The internal resources are also important considerations because the influencing of suppliers demands investments of various kinds. It is a matter of mutuality, which is also a matter of strategic conciousness[17]. The choice of supplier can often be very strategic. A long-term reason for cooperation with a certain supplier can be, for example, that a specific supplier possesses important competence which the purchasing corporation wishes to take advantage of, not only by way of a developed product but also via the corporation learning from the supplier and at an early stage receiving information of new developments, etc. The purchasing corporation can also have long-term reasons for enhancing of a certain supplier's competence.

Included in a strategic awareness of the possibilities and limitations there must also be insight into how various strategies for technological development are related to the corporation's preconditions as well as organization and personnel. An altered strategy for technological development, for example, increasing demands on the part of the supplier, normally requires both organizational as well as personnel adaptation.

The need to act and react

In respect to most corporations there is great potential opportunity in external development cooperation. These possibilities are not static, waiting to be utilized. The network is unstable and imperfect (see Chapter 3). The external actors who have the relevant resources at their disposal seek possibilities to increase the opportunities for new combinations. Certain opportunities are discovered without them being interesting or possible to utilize. Others are taken up. Many possibilities are never discovered. In the same way the purchasing corporation can be aware or unaware of the possibilities of combining an external actor's resources with its own. They may initiate technological exchange. Such initiatives, however, are not always fruitful. The suppliers can be involved in a number of activities which they do not or cannot pull out of. It can also be true that suppliers do not consider proposed technological exchange with a specific partner to be worthwhile.

In respect to the individual corporation it is, despite all the obstacles in the network, important to act and take the initiative so as to promote change. Certain possibilities can, in the long run, be worthwhile in activities which at the present are of a lower priority. This can be the case in marginal transactions with a certain supplier which as such, in the long run, create conditions which exert influence. Often, considerable knowledge and experience between the partners is needed for successful cooperation. They successively form each other in a number of dimensions and as such also the possibilities for the future. Taking the initiative and acting in respect to the supplier network is an important task in supplier management.

It is not, however, less important to react. Technological development in the industrial network includes features of both conscious systematic searching after opportunities as well as random selection. The development possibilities which should be utilized are, for this reason, dependent on which actors realize these possibilities and in what direction they wish to move, that is to say, how well a certain actor's utilization of an opportunity is adaptable with other actor's utilization of the same opportunity. Reaction in respect to these opportunities is created by both the individual as well as others' activities in the network and is for this reason equally as important as acting.

The need to control resources

For a corporation to be able to act and react, it must not only have the resources to take the initiative but must also ensure that it is attractive to others as a potential partner. The Swedish biotechnological corporation Pharmacia annually invests large sums of money in their Research and Development program, which is often relatively exploratory in nature. An important reason for this is that the corporation wants to have a body of know-how as a means of maintaining its position as an interesting partner. When an external actor has a need to complement its own resources as a means of achieving results in a development project, it is often natural for them to make contact with Pharmacia. By way of their resource position Pharmacia is open to a number of possibilities and is prepared to react.

The resources which the corporation has direct control over are the basis for acting and reacting in the network. The value of such direct and indirectly controlled resources changes over time. It is for this reason an important task in supplier management to follow the development in the network and struggle to increase control of the resources which are or will be critical[18]. At the same time it is important to cease efforts to control resources which have lost their importance. This can, however, be problematic, especially in those cases where the corporation has established control and also created a dependency in respect to certain suppliers. The building up of resource control and at the same time balancing power relationships with individual time elasticities, etc., is accordingly a very strategic task in purchasing management.[19] The control of resources gives, in conclusion, a corporation the preconditions necessary for the corporation to act and react effectively.

Notes to Chapter 4

1. For references to studies of technological development, see the introduction of Chapters 2 and 3.

2. These two cases build upon Axelsson & Håkansson, (1984). EIS is included in the business area of informations systems within Ericsson. Other business areas are Public Telecommunication, Cable, Radio Communication, Defence Systems and Network Building. Saab-Scania produces not only lorries but also buses, cars, aeroplanes and advanced electronic equipment.

3. Johanson & Mattsson (1984) use the term macro-position which has a similar meaning.

4. Johanson & Mattsson (1984) use the term micro-position when discussing positions to individual actors. In Håkansson (ed, 1982) the supplier's relation to the customer is the point of departure for a discussion of marketing strategy. The customer's relationship to the supplier is accordingly related to a disussion of purchasing strategy. The authors note a separation between the corporation's need in problem solving on a qualitative (general) level and the need for individual adaptation of the separate company. The corporation doing the purchasing has needs which can consequently be high or low, both in terms of quality as well as in relation to adaptability. Furthermore, a distinction is made in relation to the corporation's need for transference of problem solving. This is a way to - at least partly - identify a company's position in relation to individual actors.

5. For a discussion of critical resources, see Blau (1964). See also Axelsson & Håkansson (1979) where five important resource areas are distinguished, namely input material, capital, personnel, technology and marketing.

6. The company measurements and rankings were made in Veckans Affärer (The Businesses of the Week) no 25, 1983.

7. For a definition of a company buying centre, see Webster & Wind, (1972).

8. The point of departure for the research project is the structure which was at hand in the Swedish special steel industry in 1976 when a major governmental investigation was carried out. This project has partly a historical perspective. The companies which at the time were considered to be special steel companies were Avesta, Bofors, Fagersta, Gränges Nyby, Sandvik, SKF-Steel, Surahammar and Uddeholm. When this study was conducted in 1983 some major changes had taken place, but these companies still operate - at least in the shape of production units.

9. We make a distinction between net and network. In accordance with Hägg, & Johanson, (eds., 1982) we use the word net when we refer to a specific set of actors which are interrelated by relationships. The term network is used when we refer to the industrial system in a broader sense. Aldrich, & Whetten (1981) distinguishes for similar reasons between organization-sets, action- sets, and networks.

10. Axelsson & Håkansson (1984) identify three roles for purchasing. The authors claim that purchasing can contribute to a company's competitive power in three major areas; 1. It can contribute to the corporation's technological development by systematically matching the company's development to that of the suppliers. It can have a development role; 2. It can also act to lower the total cost of input materials etc., it can have a rationalization role; 3. It can also contribute by acting in a way that the company does not get into difficult situations of dependency. It can have a network role.

11. Case-hardening steels has a low amount of coal. It hardens on the surface. It aims at achieving high yield points and rupture limits.

12. Motor-car sheet steel is not regarded as a special steel but is included here to contribute to the complete picture of steel usage at Volvo.

13. Control and power are two related concepts: both can be related to re-sources. Dahl (1957) claims that 'A has power over B to the extent that he can get B to do something that B would not do otherwise'. Dahl refers to the base of power as the resources that a party can use to influence a second party's behaviour. According to Kutschker (1982) it is however important to distinguish between a base of power and the resources possessed by a party. These resources can only be translated into a base of power by a company if these resources are important to a second company.

14. Volvo owns a forge but not a special steel supplier.

15. Of course ownership does not automatically give full control over the supplier. It is only one basis for control. Dahl (1957) identifies for example six individual bases of power; reward, coercive, referent, legitimacy, expertise, and informational power. These ways of attaining indirect control over a supplier may lead to even greater control than ownership.

16. Two different methods of approach can hereby be contemplated, namely P-centric and set-centric analyses. As Kutschker (1982, p. 377) explains 'P-centric analysis reduces the complexity of multilateral relationships by decomposing the network into a number of bilateral relationships'. While 'the set-centric' approach views all of the relationships in a network simultaneously, which should ensure the comprehension of the multilaterality of relationships (ibid. p. 378). Kutschker claims that there does not exist any direct opposite relationship between these methods of approach. They can, for example, both be viewed from the perspective of resource control.

17. For a discussion of mutuality in buyer-seller relationships, see Ford et al. (1985).

171

18. The critical issue is as a matter of fact to achieve this control before the resource has been critical, afterwards it is too expensive.

19. For a distinction between the relationship between power and dependence, see Galbraith (1952) and Goldman (1978). Goldman distinguishes between offensive power and defensive. Offensive power refers to the power of one actor over the others, while defensive power refers to the company's ability to avoid the control of other actors.

Appendix 1

The companies and their activity patterns.

Five of the 14 investigated corporations work selectively/continually. These are Alfa-Laval, Sandvik Saws and Tools, ESAB, SKF and ASEA, all of which have intensive relationships with certain special steel suppliers. With these suppliers they also have, for the most part, ongoing technological exchange. Even Volvo Cars, Saab-Scania and Atlas Copco have ongoing technological exchange with special steel producers, but these corporations work on a broader basis. They have several development project relationships which they utilize, all of which are on nearly the same level. Three of these 14 corporations work selectively/discontinually; these are Stal-Laval Turbin, Saab Aeroplane and Volvo Aero-Engines. there are also three corporations which operate broadly/continually; these are Sunds Defibrator, ÖMV and Kema Nobel.

In reference to Alfa-Laval, whose main product line is separators and heat-exchangers, special steel is a very important material, especially for the so-called centrifugal separators. The main components in these separators is the separator forging. This component is exposed to excessive stress partly because of the separator's high rotational velocity, and also because of the pressure which the lubricant is operating under at separation; approximately 5 000 Rpm (rotation per minute). The lubricant is also often corrosive. The forge determines both what type of separation is possible and the effectiveness of the separation process. The most important demands on the material are strength in combination with corrosion resistance.

Special steel forged products are thus very critical components. Their importance can be traced in a wide range of the production cycle. That the special steel supplier's transformation activities are very important for Alfa-Laval can be traced to the fact that Alfa-Laval's products are very important for the customer's production. They influence the customer's performance, as well as the customer's potential performance. The separation forging is for this reason a vital concern for a large number of corporations on several levels in the production network.

In respect to ESAB, a welding company, the contact with the special steel producers has two central aspects. The producers are the suppliers of welding wire to ESAB, while at the same time they are the producers of products which need to be welded. Even for this corporation special steel is of primary importance for the user's products. ESAB's ability to compete is decided by how they can succeed in solving their customers' welding problems. The use of materials

172

also in this case has an importance which extends over several of the transformation and transaction cycles.

Sandvik Saws and Tools considers special steel to be a critical resource. The most important problem in respect to materials in this company is the difficulty of combining toughness with hardness. The corporation has, for this reason, developed a bi-metal material. Instead of making the saw blade completely out of high-speed steel, which is relatively fragile, the company uses ESR based welding to weld together a tough base material with a hard tooth material. Even in this case special steel is important in several transaction and transformation cycles.

In respect to ASEA, a corporation which among other things produces electric motors and systems for generation and transmission of electrical power, special steel is not generally seen to be equally as important. The so called orientation of electro-steel is, however, a feature which is important for certain of ASEA's products.

For SKF, a company which produces various types of ball bearings, special steel is important for both the production process and the product line.

All of the corporations, Alfa-Laval, ESAB, Sandvik Saws and Tools, ASEA and SKF cooperate on a selective and continual basis with special steel corporations. These developmental activities are carried on continuously, even if the intensity at times varies. The activities are directed primarily towards one or a limited number of suppliers, who are very important external development resources.

In relation to Volvo and Saab-Scania, whose main products are automobiles and lorries respectively, special steel is less important for the end-product. To a great extent the materials question is related to the fact that materials must satisfy certain demands which are considered as restrictions. An important goal is, however , that these demands should be met by a material which weighs as little as possible. Also, the material should be as inexpensive as possible. The development activities which these users deal with together with the special steel producers are dominated by technical production problems, with among other things, machinability as an important aspect. Other important improvements can and have been realized by the simplification of heat treatment, limited usage of expensive material, etc. The materials function for the user is primarily to ease transaction activities with consumers through lower prices.

In relation to Atlas Copco, a corporation which produces rock drilling equipment, special steel is also of limited importance. The material must satisfy certain minimum demands. Development activities with special steel producers are primarily related to production improvements.

These corporations, Volvo, Saab-Scania and Atlas Copco, work with a larger group of special steel suppliers. The spokesman of Saab-Scania says that they have *ongoing and extensive joint development projects with many different special steel producers*. These development activities are composed primarily of modifications and adaptations of the supplier's product so as to satisfy the user's specific needs. The developmental activities are important primarily as a means of 'keeping up' with technological development. The special steel producers are widely used, and the corporations have a long line of development partners.

In respect to Stal-Laval Turbin, a corporation which produces marine turbines and so called stationary steam and gas turbines for power stations, special steel plays an important role in relation to the competitive standing of the company's products. The performance of the turbines is determined to a large degree by the heat resistive qualities of the components which are subjected to high levels of stress at high temperatures. The feature which is critical is for this reason strength at high temperatures. In respect to Stal-Laval, as well as ESAB and

Sandvik Saws and Tools, materials quality has importance over the entire transformation cycle. It is not only the transaction activities with Stal-Laval's customers which are influenced, but also their transformation activities and consequent transactions.

In respect to Volvo Aero-engines, a company which produces components for aero engines and is included in the so-called aviation net, and Saab Aeroplanes, which produces fuselages, special steel plays, in a larger perspective, a relatively limited role. Other materials, such as titanium and various super alloys are more important.

Unlike the corporations mentioned above, Stal-Laval Turbin, Volvo Aero-Engines and Saab Aeroplanes all work selectively but not equally as ongoing with the special steel producers. This depends, most likely, to a large extent on the corporation's production technology. These companies develop and produce air-planes and turbines in intensive production periods. In connection with larger projects, such as the development of a new generation of products, the contacts become more intensive. In connection with various other projects, however, there is a selection. Certain suppliers are given priority over others. Stal-Laval expressed this idea as such; *the most common method at the start of a new project is to contact the established suppliers and if they are uninterested, to continue looking without preconceptions.* Consequently, the established procedure is to seek out and utilize those external resources which one has had experience with and which can best contribute to the solving of the corporation's problems.

Kema Nobel is the only process corporation among the 14. They produce, among other things, raw materials for plastics manufacturing. In respect to Kema Nobel, special steel is relevant to their production equipment in two ways. First off, special steel is present in the equipment which is procured; for example, heat converters, boilers, large vessels, tubing, etc. In these cases the corporation's demands, in relation to materials, are directed primarily towards those mechanical engineering companies which deliver the equipment. Special steel is also actualized when the corporation needs replacement materials; here the order is often placed directly with the special steel producer.

Special steel thus has a long-term importance for Kema Nobel's transformation and transaction activities with its customers through better production effectiveness. The life-length of the material can be easier to estimate, which is important. Besides, the propensities e.g. corrosion resistance, can be improved. Thus, components last longer and can be replaced in an optimal manner; not too early and not too late.

Sunds Defibrator and ÖMV deliver equipment to process corporations in the chemical, and the pulp and paper fields. Special steel is important both for their products and for their customer's production.

All of these latter corporations referred to, Kema Nobel, Sunds Defibrator and ÖMV, work widely with a large group of special steel producers; (primarily with stainless steel products). They operate discontinuously. Their need for new materials is well known by the steel producers. There is a very large group of other users who have similar needs. These three corporations contribute to the development primarily through the increase in demand for these types of products.

174

Appendix 2

The Swedish Special Steel Industry; The Products, the Producers, the Application Areas and, the Most Important Swedish Users. (The matrix is based, to a large extent, on the Swedish Steel Manual, Jernkontoret, 1981.)

Steel	Main Swedish producer 1981	Examples of applications	Examples of important Swedish users
1. Tool Steels a) High Speed Steels — bars and wires	Kloster Speed Steel	Cutting tools	Wedevågs bruk, Granlunds, Sandvik Coromant, SKF Tools
— strips	Kloster Speed Steel	Machine saw blades	Sandvik Saws and Tools, Kapman
b) Hot work tool steels	Uddeholm Tooling	Tools for press forgings	Small tool manufacturers. End users within the automobile industry
c) Cold work tool steels	Uddeholm Tooling	Cutting tools	As for hot work tool steels
d) Rock drill steels	Fagersta, Sandvik	Rock drilling tools	Sandvik Coromant, Seco Roc
2. Stainless Steels a) Bars	Avesta, Sandvik Nyby-Uddeholm	Constructions	Wide spread usage within the mechanical engineering industry
b) Cold rolled bands and strips	Fagersta, Sandvik, Uddeholm	Chemical-, pulp and paper, food industry. Heat-exchangers, boilers, but also various household articles.	Alfa-Laval, Electrolux, IFÖ-verken, Bulten-Kanthal, Gustafsberg, Sandvik, Sandvik Saws and Tools
c) Hot rolled plates and sheets	Avesta, Uddeholm	As for cold rolled bands and strips; chemical-, pulp- and paper-, food industry	As for cold rolled plates and sheets, but also Sunds Defibrator, KMV, ASEA-Atom, ÖMV, Uddcomb
d) Wire (hot rolled, cold drawn, welding wire, electrodes)	Avesta, Fagersta, Sandvik, Uddeholm, Gunnebo-Uddeholm Stainless AB	The drawn wire is used in e.g. the manufacturing of refrigerators	End-users in the machine shop industry, Bulten-Kanthal, Brusaholm, ESAB, Siemens, Monark
e) Tubes (seamless, welded, fabricated)	Avesta, Fagersta, Sandvik, Uddeholm	As for cold rolled bands and strips	Alfa-Laval, MoDo, Iggesund, Sunds Defibrator, Götaverken Ångteknik, Hedemora verkstäder, Kema Nobel

Steel	Main Swedish producer 1981	Examples of applications	Examples of important Swedish users
f) Forgings			
— hammer and press forgings	Avesta, Surahammar, Uddeholm	Equipment for chemical industries, but also separator forgings	As for tubes
— drop and precision forgings	Bofors	Precision forging for the aviation industry	Stal-Laval Turbin, Volvo Aeroengine
g) Castings	Fagersta, Uddeholm	Components for equipment in the process industry	SCA, Kema Nobel
h) High temperature alloys	Fagersta, Sandvik, Uddeholm	As for castings	As for castings
3. Alloyed construction (toughhardening, spring, ballbearing, magnet steels)	Fagersta, Sandvik, SKF Steel, Surahammar	Components for automobile and other machine shop industries	Volvo, Saab-Scania, Atlas Copco, Stal-Laval Turbin, SKF
4. Plates and sheets			
— electrical silicon sheets	Surahammar	Transformers, electrical engines	ASEA
5. Tubes and tubular products (constructional tubes, ball bearing tubes)	Sandvik, SKF Steel, Uddeholm	Process equipment, boiler tubes in power plants, manufacturing of ball bearings	Process industry, machine shop industry (see stainless tubes)
6. Strip steel and flat wire, cold rolled			
— spring steel	Fagersta, Sandvik, Uddeholm	Spring manufacture for use in e.g. security belts in automobiles	See stainless wire
— band saw steel for metal and wood	Sandvik, Uddeholm Strip Steel	Saws	Sandvik Saws and Tools, Westlings Saw Blade Manufacture, Stridsbergs & Björk, Brusaholm, Munkfors Saws, etc.
— magnet iron	Sandvik, SKF Steel	Telephones	Ericsson
— electrical resistance material	Sandvik, SKF Steel	Electronics	ASEA, Ericsson
7. Cold finished bars and wire (construction components, carbon welding wire, piano wire etc.)	Fagersta, Sandvik, SKF Steel	Manufacturing of ball bearings, piano wire, etc.	SKF, Manufacturers of string instruments

Chapter Five

TECHNOLOGICAL DEVELOPMENT AND THE INDIVIDUAL'S CONTACT NETWORK

Cecilia Hamfelt and Ann-Kristin Lindberg

The Importance of Personal Contacts

The smallest threads in the industrial network run between individuals. It is the individual who makes contact, becomes acquainted, and builds up trust between companies. One basic requirement for technological exchange and the development of the contact network is thus that there are people within the corporation who initiate and develop these contacts.

The personal contacts are at the heart of interaction between organizations, (Cunningham & Turnbull, 1982, p. 314). Personal contacts are the medium in which communication takes place. Direct contact between individuals is especially important for the forms of information exchange which often occur in relation to technological development. The network's perspective in respect to technological development accentuates certain aspects of the importance of personal contact's. There are three such aspects which shall be discussed. First the individual as a discoverer of possibilities. Secondly, the individual as an information transmitter and thirdly the individual as a resource mobilizer.

Commercial and technological exchange between corporations in industrial markets is in accordance with the network approach distinguished to a large extent by repetitive activity cycles. The buyer orders, the seller produces and attends to transportation, the buyer stores, produces, orders, etc. The most dominant work is conducted in similarly repetitive patterns.

Sometimes there occur 'special events' in this daily work; for example, a crucial delay in delivery, personnel changes, or attempts to develop and introduce new technologies. Everyday occurrences are, however, quite often not only a string of identical events. Each individual event can create what in time is experienced as a 'special event.'[1]

Because technological development is characterized by both systematic and chance occurrences, and developmental possibilities often slip in by the daily routine, the individual has the important task of utilizing those opportunities which often quickly disappear.[2] An individual's 'fingerspitzgefühl' is vital in respect to the opportunities which are utilized both within the corporation as well as in the external network.

The individual as an information transmitter has earlier been given attention both in relation to the external network as well as in respect to internal networks. In Czepiel (1974), it is described, for example, as the information diffusion process with a communication network approach. In this approach such factors as word-of-mouth, opinion leadership, information gatekeepers, initiation and contact diffusion are important in understanding the rate and direction of innovation diffusion. Based on data obtained from sociometric questions concerning various information sources and their frequency of use, Czepiel explores the existence of 'informal societies' in two different industrial settings, the steel industry and the electrical utilities industry. One conclusion is that a study of the innovation process must include the social environment and this includes not only the internal organization of the company but also the outside organization, suppliers, customers and competitors as well.

In Allen (1977) the focus is on the individual as an information transmitter in the internal network. One of the author's main points is that information from the organization's external environment affects individual technicians in the first phase by way of key people, so called 'gatekeepers'. The internal contact structure is based on certain central people who relay their knowledge to their colleagues, who for differing reasons have less developed external contacts. The spreading of information, which can also be related to the discussion of 'fingerspitzgefühl' has also been studied by, among others, Menzel (1967). The author claims that some advantages with personal communication compared with written communication is that the information is selected and evaluated in a better manner. It is easier to formulate abstract knowledge relevant to measures taken in terms adaptable to specific receivers, as well as local conditions.

Because technological development, to a large extent, deals with handling information, it is naturally the individual's role as an information transmitter in the network which is of central importance. The tasks of a corporation are not only to transmit or sort out information but also to confirm and spread knowledge about technological information. A Swedish chemical company, Perstorp, has, for example, a number of engineers whose main task is to follow the technological development which occurs within the corporation's field. The aim is to gather information and convey such to the operative divisions.

A third concern which complements the others is the individual's role in actively mobilizing and organizing the network's resources. Contacts, knowledge and confidence are three key words in this connection. An individual with one or several of these qualities can increase a company's ability in this respect considerably. Contacts and knowledge will not be discussed any more here as they are very similar to the issues discussed above. Confidence, however, needs some comment. To mobilize resources one must ask others to raise money, manpower or some other resource for a business venture with an uncertain outcome. To do this in a successful way requires confidence, i.e. the other must have trust in the ability of the suggester.

The Individual and the Corporation as Active Network Participants

In Rogers and Larsen (1984) there is a discussion of information exchanges within the micro-electronic industry in Silicon Valley. The authors relay the manner in which an engineer regards the network of corporations in that area. The engineer said,

> *I know someone, and they know someone, but I don't know who they know. The power of this network is that the participants all know it exists. We all know that we all know lots of other people in the Valley. This is mainly due to the rate of mobility. the rate of rumor-passing in Silicon Valley is simple phenomenal. Reputations, successes, people leaving a firm, new products. The mill grinds out these rumors at a prodigious rate. (ibid., p. 80).*

The individual participates in the network and can also exploit it. He or she can act as active network participants.

It has already been stated that the smallest threads in the industrial network run between individuals. The individuals, however, are multi-dimensional and have many roles in the total network. One can, for example, over and above one's occupation, be a member of a professional association (doctors, buyers, metallurgical engineers, etc.), or a member of a voluntary group such as Rotary[3]. The individual as such, in their network, can function in many roles. The manner in which they utilize the network can for this reason have many purposes. The individual corporation's total contact network is naturally related to those contact networks which these employees operate in. The corporation consists of a number of individual networks. But because the individual maintains several roles, the corporation consists in actual terms of a collection of roles. This line of reasoning indicates that there are some very important differences between individuals and corporations in respect to their active network participation. The individual can utilize the network as a means of building up his position in two distinctive ways.[4] Firstly, one can successively build up a contact network for the position one finds oneself in. Secondly, one can utilize the network in order to jump from position to position. From a corporate perspective, this 'mobile one' can either be of an internal or an external type. Regardless of which network structure is discussed, such jumping can, at the same time, be influenced by several of the individual's roles.

Even the separate company can, as an active network participant, act in at least two distinct and different ways. It can try to keep the existing individuals together and let them develop their contact networks. Alternatively it can actively 'import' and 'export' people with certain experience. The corporation can recruit in such a way that it receives access to interesting contact networks and it can try to influence individuals within the company to get new jobs in units where their knowledge of the company can be of value.[5]

The Study

As a means of attaining a picture of a contact network which develops in an industrial network, 426 engineers' technological contacts both internal and external were investigated.[6] The fundamental idea is that the contact networks which are developed by a key group of individuals within a network - in this case the Swedish special steel network - should reflect how the network functions. It should give a picture of which units are more or less closely related to each other. They should also indicate which type of external and internal actors are most central from, for example, a developmental point of view. They should reflect how integrated the corporations are among themselves, with different external actors and with different internal functions. Such phenomena and patterns on the individual level should consequently reflect the conditions on a superior level.

The engineers studied comprise a specific group of professionals. All of them are metallurgical engineers. This group of professionals is distinguished by the fact that they all have a similar education, common traditions, and are considered as a professional 'club'. Metallurgical engineers are without doubt the most central vocational group within the special steel industry. Among the technicians studied, 32% worked in special steel and 12% in commercial steel corporations. The remaining 56% are spread out in other fields as is seen in Figure 5:1.

Approximately 20% work in corporations which are within the engineering industry; mechanical engineering firms, suppliers to the steel industry, etc. Examples of corporations within the remaining industries are producers of rock-drills and components for power stations. The remaining corporate types are designated in the figure. The study has consequently been limited to a group of professionals active within a large number of corporations and fields with a clear interest in the special steel industry.

Metallurgical engineers are widely spread out in the hierarchy of positions within a company. In Table 5:1 it is shown how such positions are distributed within the special steel industry.

Here it is seen that positions within production, R&D, corporate management, and marketing are the most common.

The analysis is to be centered on the engineers who work within the special steel industry and in the four main types of

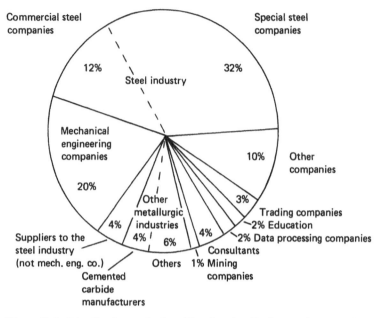

Figure 5:1 Distribution of the Metallurgic Engineers in regard to Company Type.

vocational positions. In the study, the professional group's technonogical contacts, both external and internal, have been examined. These contact patterns have been mapped out as a mean average, that is to say, as a measurement of the every-day

Table 5:1 Working Position of the Metallurgic Engineers within the Special Steel Companies.

R&D	31
Production	33
Quality control	7
Design	1
Project/research	6
Marketing	19
Customer service	6
Corporate management	16
Administration	5
Purchasing	6
Patent	3
Others	1
	134

182

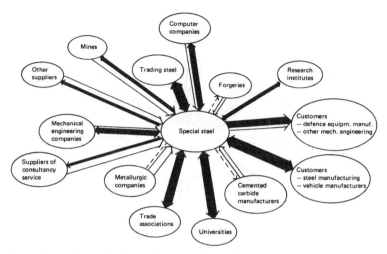

Note: The width of the arrows illustrates the number of surveyed engineers who have contact with every organization represented. The widest arrows represent more than 60% of the engineers surveyed. The solid part of the arrows illustrate contacts which mining engineers in special steel companies have with external organizations.

Figure 5:2 Contacts of Metallurgic Engineers in different Companies.

activities and not of special occurrences. These contact patterns shall indicate main points of importance in the network. The contacts are discussed in terms of partners, content, form and scope. The interpretations and explanations for similarities and variations in the contact pattern are found primarily in the properties of the individual; rank, experience, and education, the qualities of the corporation including size, and the characteristics of the network.

The Network - an Overview

Metallurgical engineers in the special steel industry have technological contacts with a large number of organizations in the industrial network. A large number of contacts with these external units are directly related to the special steel industry. This is illustrated in Figure 5:2.

A large number of contacts originate in the steel industry. Most of the engineers have forward contacts with customers, back-

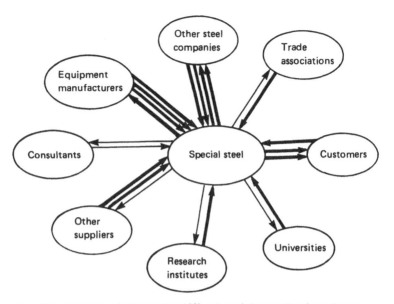

Note: The small arrow indicates that 10% or less of the metallurgic engineers considered that external organization to be the most important from a technological perspective. The solid arrows represent 10% to 20% of the engineers.

Figure 5:3 Important Technological Contacts According to the Engineers.

ward contacts with suppliers and vertical contacts with lateral actors such as research institutes. Many engineers in the external units have in turn some form of exchange with the steel corporations. This is primarily important for those who work in supply and customer companies. Almost all of the engineers in supply companies have forward contacts with the steel industry while considerably fewer in the special steel companies have backward contacts with the suppliers. Forward contacts in the production chain are dominant.

Those types of corporations and organizations which, from a technological viewpoint, are most important for the special steel industry are illustrated in Figure 5:3.

The direction of the arrows indicates that the forward contacts in the production chain are very important, while contacts backwards to various types of suppliers are not as highly valued. There are consequently relatively few engineers in the steel industry who consider that equipment suppliers are the most important contact partner. Contact with customers such as, for example, mechanical engineering firms, are considered, on the other hand, as being to a large extent very important.

If we instead begin with the equipment suppliers, contacts with steel corporations are clearly dominant. The steel industry makes up an important group of customers. In the same way the main body of metallurgical engineers within the mechanical engineering companies consider their customers as being very important. Even within this group far fewer representatives who responded to this study have contact with suppliers such as, for example, steel companies.

The understanding of the essential part of the contact structure can, however, be found to go off in various directions depending upon what vocational position we center our approach. Research organizations probably do not have the same subordinate role if the researchers' contacts are studied. In the same way contacts with equipment suppliers should most likely be considered more important if we begin with for example production personnel's contact network. One can consequentely expect high priority contacts with individual actors dependent on what positions these actors have.

We shall now begin a closer study of the four dominant groups; corporate leaders, marketing executives, researchers and production personnel, and their respective contact network.

Metallurgical Engineers within Corporate Management

The special steel industry in Sweden, which earlier often consisted of smaller family owned companies, is today comprised of a few large, global corporations. The corporate management of these corporations has changed as a result of this development. The work tasks, which earlier were handled by a factory owner who had sole control, now demand several people.

It has been seen in our study that 16 engineers are corporate managers in the handful of corporations which today comprise the Swedish special steel industry. Five of these 16 engineers are corporate presidents, three are vice presidents, six are division managers and two are managers of profit centers. A large number of this industry's corporate managers are metallurgical engineers. In a survey of the leading personnel within the special steel industry, Bergqvist, Hamfelt and Lindberg (1983) found that between 60 and 70% of the special steel corporation's presidents during 1970 to 1975 were members of the metallurgical engineer profession.

The majority of engineers in corporate management in our study were recruited internally. Roughly 30% have at all times or during long periods worked within their respective corporation. Among the 16 it was most common that their earlier position had been in corporate management. On the other hand, most of these people had, earlier on in their careers, been involved in other areas, such as research or production.

The management of a corporation is traditionally responsible for the company's profile and strategic planning. An extensive contact and information network is certainly an important precondition for successfully meeting these demands.

Corporate management and their technological contacts

The corporate managers studied all have a wide external contact network, as can be seen in Figure 5:4. All except one, for example, have technological contacts with customer companies. Nine of the corporate leaders consider these contacts to be the most important. All of the corporate leaders futhermore have contacts with representatives of other Swedish steel companies. These contacts are considered as being important, however, only two consider them to be the most important. In a rank-ordering of the importance of certain contacts, approximately a third of the corporate leaders have indicated that contacts with other steel companies are of secondary importance. Most of the managers have furthermore technological contacts with equipment suppliers, and approximately half of them consider that these contacts are important. On the other hand none of them have indicated that these are the most important contacts.

The differences lie, consequently, in an estimation of the most important external contacts. This can depend on the steel company one works for, their area of activity and history, but it can also be influenced by the corporate leader's earlier experience.

We shall attempt to come to terms with this by making a special study of the group of corporate leaders who considered

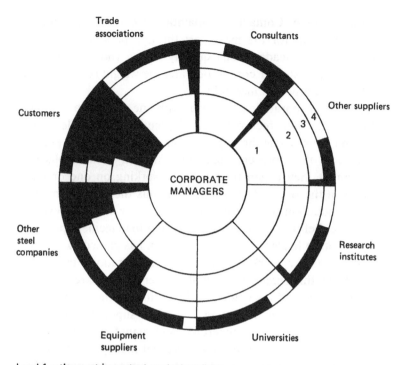

Level 1 = the most important contact partner
Level 2 = one of the two most important contact partners
Level 3 = one of the three most important contact partners
Level 4 = have established contact
(Shadowed areas indicate degree of established contact.)

Figure 5:4 The Contact Network of the Corporate Managers.

customer contacts to be most important. Following this the remaining corporate leaders will be discussed.

Customer contacts

Ten corporate leaders in the study considered customer contacts to be the most important. These ten people can roughly be divided into two equally large groups in respect to the contact structure. The first group meets with colleagues who hold corporate leadership positions in the customer corporations while the other group primarily has contact with technical people. For the first group it is important that besides the corporate leaders they also meet other personnel categories such as technicians, buyers and sales people. Contacts are maintained one or more times a week and occur for the most part through personal meetings. These corporate leaders consequently have a wide area of contact with the customer corporation and the weight rests at a high point in the corporate hierarchy.

All of the corporate leaders have, with one exception, a similar background. They received their degree in the middle of the 1960s and either came directly, or after a few years at a research institute, to their present company. At their present place of employment they began their careers working on one or more projects in the research division. After this they have gone over to the production and project department, in one case even to marketing, before they received their first management position. The corporate leader who is an exception has gained experience and contacts by working for several corporations in various fields. Even this engineer began his career at a research institute after he completed his degree in the middle of the 1950s. Afterwards he worked in marketing as both a supplier to the steel industry and within a commercial steel manufacturer. The last three years before he received his present management position he held a management position in a customer company. Most likely many of the important customer contacts which he now has consist of conversations with old work colleagues. From a recruitment perspective this is an interesting example of the hiring of personnel with an established external network.

The four corporate leaders who have extensive external networks and who have worked in their present company also have extensive internal contact exchange. Mainly, they converse with other personnel in corporate management, however, a large number of contacts occur with other departments.

Against the background of these people's wide contact network, both external as well as internal, we can assume that they function as important channels of information. At the same time, broad contact exchange is a precondition for the managements' ability to be able to follow in what direction possible changes are going and anticipate what opportunities as such are open to their own corporations.

The second group consists of engineers who also consider customer contacts to be important but who primarily have important relations with the customer corporations' technological departments. Contacts are made once every month or so and occur almost exclusively through personal meetings.

This group's contact exchange is not as intensive as the group first discussed. The contacts are of a more specific nature and are conducted when technological questions and problems must be discussed. The first group's technological contacts are most likely of a more fundemantal and broader nature. For both groups, developing problem solving techniques, as well as cooperation with their customers in technological questions, are both strategic tasks.

One of the corporate leaders in this group has worked for the same firm since taking his degree in the middle of the 50s. The other engineers have, in all cases, worked in other corporations up until the middle of the 1970s. In their previous firms they have held positions within their respective corporation's technological departments. In all, this second group of corporate leaders has a smaller contact network with the customer corporations compared to the first group. Their careers are also more dominated by experience in technological departments.

The internal contact pattern is, on the other hand, not very different in the two groups. It is possible that contacts with corporate leadership are emphasized to a somewhat greater extent in the first group. Primarily, all of the engineers have a very broad and extensive internal contact network within their own corporate unit.

Contacts with other external units

Of the remaining six corporate leaders, four maintain that other external organizations are important in respect to technology while two leaders have not been able or preferred not to choose one specific type of external organization as being the most important. Two corporate leaders maintain that relations with consultants in respective trade associations and two that contacts with other Swedish steel corporations are the most important. The latter named people's earlier experiences are similar, despite the fact that they represent two different ways to achieve a top position within the corporate structure. One of the engineers received his degree in the middle of the 1950s and has during the entirety of his career worked for the same corporation. He can be said to have gone 'the long hard way'. His career began in research and production, followed by a period in the company's marketing department. Following this period he has been, since the middle of the 1970s, in corporate management. In the steel corporations this engineer has contacts with representatives of the marketing department.

The second engineer has a similar background and experience; he has, however, received this experience in a different corporation, a commercial steel company. During the five years preceding his current management position he was a division manager at the steel company. Following this he was recruited and promoted to his current management position.

The two people's internal contact networks are quite different from each other. The corporate leader who has always worked in the same corporation has a very wide internal contact network with most of the functions within his own unit. The other corporate leader's internal contacts are limited to relations with the corporation's division managers, as well as managers in the subsidiaries. He also has contacts with the corporation's union officials.

Concluding comments - metallurgical engineers as corporate leaders

The corporate leaders (who are also metallurgical engineers), have a personal contact network which is recognized primarily by its extensiveness. This occupational group has in common a wide contact structure both internally and externally. Extensiveness of the internal contacts is dependent, among other things, on the fact that the engineers have generally worked for a long time in their current company and have also been involved in various roles.

The external group which these corporate leading engineers consider most important from a technological perspective is without doubt the customer.

Metallurgical Engineers in R&D

In the survey 31 engineers worked within the research departments of the special steel industry. This is one fourth of the total number of surveyed people in the special steel industry. These engineers have in most cases worked for a relatively long time in their present company, on an average, since the middle of the 1960s. Many worked, even before their present position, in the present corporation and even at that time in research. Twelve of the 31 engineers have, during the entirety of their careers been loyal to one and the same corporation. The remaining 19 have at some earlier date worked for other companies or organizations. This has as such most often been research institutions and/or steel companies. These are employments which in most cases occurred a considerable time in the past; for the most part ten years or more. One of the people was recruited during the last of the surveyed years. Even in this case there had been earlier employment in another steel company. In all there are only four people who have been recruited directly from other corporations to the position they hold today. Three of these came from other steel companies while one came from a position at a research institute. It is consequently most common that they have had at least one other term of employment within the same corporation before filling their present position.

External contacts

Certain types of the researchers' contacts are especially common, for example contacts with other steel corporations, trade associations, universities as well as research institutes (see Figure 5:5). It is with these corporations and organizations which one in general expects research personnel to have contact. There are, on the other hand, not as many as might be expected who have forward contacts with their customers. It can also be seen, however, that most of those who have customer contacts consider this to be important. Many researchers have considered the customers to be the most important contact partner.

Despite the fact that almost all of the engineers have contact with industry organizations and universities, only a few have expressed the fact that these organizations belong to one of the three important contact partners. Those organizations which dominate in this respect are the steel corporations, customers and research institutes. The customers clearly dominate among the units which are perceived to be most important. There are comparatively fewer who consider the steel corporations or the research institutes to be their first consideration. Contacts with

191

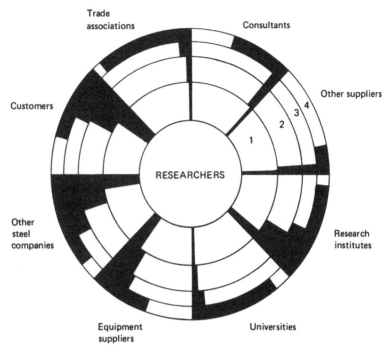

Level 1 = the most important contact partner
Level 2 = one of the two most important contact partners
Level 3 = one of the three most important contact partners
Level 4 = have established contact
(Shadowed areas indicate degree of established contact.)

Figure 5:5 The Contact Network of the Researchers.

equipment suppliers are also distinguished. Only half of the researchers have contacts with this type of supplier, however, among these it has been expressed that they are important and in several cases the most important contact partner.

In the following sections we shall concentrate on the most important partner, the inner ring in Figure 5:5, and investigate these contacts as well as those engineers who have them.

Customer contacts

Eight of the 31 engineers in research consider contacts with customers most important. Within this group, all except one works in product and materials development. These are areas where the customer's attitudes and demands play an important role. Continual adjustments most likely occur according to the customer's desires, something which causes contact with the customer to be an important part of these engineers' daily duties.

The fact that contact with the customer corporation is an important aspect in the engineer's work is supported by the fact that they occur often - in a few cases they are daily contacts - otherwise once or more a week. Often contacts take the form of meetings where discussions are held among technological personnel. Firstly, other researchers are contacted, but even contact with production personnel, as well as other groups of technicians, are common.

Two of these 8 engineers have a limited contact network in repect to the customer corporation. These two contact researchers in their discussions with the customer corporation. Also, the have worked exclusively in research and they belong to a younger section of the surveyed group.

Six of the engineers have wide contact networks. They have worked externally as well as internally and with tasks other then research, or they have, as is the case for one of the above, worked internally but as such within various fields. One example is a person who has personal contact with various occupational designations on a daily basis within project and service functions at a customer corporation. This person has wide vocational experience behind him; research institute, cemented carbide producing company, as well as a special steel company, besides the firm which presently employs him. This background has created a wide contact network which is helpful and has surely been an asset in respect to present customer contact. He himself considers his work in the cemented carbide company to have been the most important in relation to his present position.

Those researchers who have customers as their most important contact partners have relatively extensive internal contacts. All of the engineers surveyed have ongoing contacts with other research and marketing personnel. Many have contacts with production personnel as well as other categories of technicians. Contacts with corporate leaders are also common. One does not only have contacts within one's own organizational unit, quite often there are contacts with other divisions as well as with subsidiaries.

There is no positive correlation between the width of external and internal contact networks. It instead appears that those who only have contacts with researchers at the customer corporation have contacts with comparatively more personnel categories in their own corporation. At the same time those with wider contact networks in respect to the customer have contacts with much fewer internal personnel categories.

Equipment supplier contacts

In the section above it was found that it was above all metallurgical engineers who are busy with product and/or material development who consider customer contact as an important part of their work. Of the six engineers who have designated equipment suppliers as their first choice, it has been found that they work for the most part with process development. Two have important leadership positions which include responsibility for process development departments. In other words, most of them (5 of 6) have direct insights into the problems which arise during the development of existing production processes, as well as in the implementation of new processes. In this type of work the suppliers of equipment are an important information source.

In all, eleven of the engineers within the R&D of the special steel industry work primarily with process development. Those of them who do not consider contact with equipment suppliers as being the most important have instead often mentioned research institutions and steel corporations as their most important contact partners. This indicates that other types of organizations and corporations can also be important sources of knowledge in the development of existing and/or new processes.

Contacts with equipment suppliers occur, compared with customer contacts, somewhat less often. One does not personally meet with representatives for equipment suppliers as often as one meets customer representatives.

In respect to contact with equipment suppliers, many discussions are conducted with research and marketing personnel. Otherwise, contacts are made with various categories of technicians, foremost with the supplier's designing department. The communication with equipment suppliers take three different forms. One group of engineers consists of those who only discuss with sales personnel. Another group is made up of those three engineers who only have contact with technicians, and lastly one group consists of engineers who have contacts with both technicians and sales personnel.

Other contacts

Besides those who have replied that customer and equipment suppliers are their most important contact partners, there were also a number of engineers who designated other types of corporations and organizations. There are, for example, three engineers who consider other steel corporations as the most important partners. All of these engineers have earlier worked in research, two internally and the third in another steel corporation other than that in which he is currently employed.

Concluding comments - metallurgical engineers in R&D

Those metallurgical engineers who work in research within the special steel industry have worked a relatively long time for their present employer; often more than ten years. Many have, during the entirety of their careers, been loyal to the same corporation. Those who have worked for other corporations have for the most part been employed in the steel industry. In those singular cases where one has worked in other industries it has been a question of closely related fields, such as mechanical engineering, where steel is an important raw material. It is considerably more common within this vocational group, as compared with other groups, that they began their careers with a few years at a research institute.

There are two types of corporations which dominate among those considered to be the most important from a technical perspective. These are customer corporations and equipment suppliers. In respect to customer contacts one talks with technological personnel; half converse with researchers, otherwise it is a question of talks with personnel within production.

Contacts with equipment suppliers occur, on the other hand, either with marketing and sales personnel or with various groups of technicians. None of the engineers, however, have close contact with the supplier's research personnel.

A number of engineers included in the study are employed in the research departments of customers to the special steel companies. Some of these feel that contacts backwards in the production chain with steel suppliers are important. There is, however, only one person among them who has contact with re-searchers, otherwise, steel corporation contacts take place with other technological personnel as well as with personnel in marketing research and sales. On the other hand, studies of the engineers within the customer corporation's research departments show that forward contact with customers is important; it is thus seen that the contacts have, in almost all the cases, been conducted with researchers. It is obviously true that forward contacts in the production chain, in respect to engineers within research, regardless of the industry, most often are made with research personnel while backward contacts are conducted with other technological personnel or with personnel within marketing and sales.

Roughly half of the engineers within the special steel industry's research programs are represented in the customer and supplier contacts described above. The remaining also have these types of contacts, but they have indicated that some other external organization is more important. These engineers have, to a great extent, contact with researchers at those organizations which they have indicated as most important. This is especially true in respect to those who have contacts with various types of research organizations.

Metallurgical Engineers within Production

In order to meet the customer's demands and desires, continual modification of existing products, as well as products under development, must be maintained. In order to manage this task continual contact with the customers is naturally demanded. Also, contact with different suppliers is needed. It is usually believed that customer contacts are conducted by the marketing functions by way of the customer's purchasing departments. Often, however, the production section is brought into the picture. Contacts are made directly between the corporations' production departments without interference of the purchasing or marketing functions.

Twentyfive percent, or 33 engineers, employed in the special steel industry's production departments, are included in this survey of metallurgical engineers. Many of these engineers have worked in the same corporation since the end of the 1960s. Most commonly they have earlier had one or a few other positions within production. Many have also, earlier in their careers, worked in research. One third of the group (11 people), have, during the entirety of their careers, worked for the same corporation, while the remaining engineers have earlier been employed at one or more other corporations. These positions were most commonly held at other steel corporations, however, in many cases they were mechanical engineering companies. Some of the engineers have worked one or more years at a research institute. This has only occurred directly after the receiving of their degree. Compared with engineers in the research field one can say that this type of employment is less common among the engineers employed in production.

Two of the engineers have come directly to their present position from other corporations. One of them has earlier worked in the steel industry while the other has, among other things, worked in the mechanical engineering field.

External contacts

There are some corporate and organization types which one expects the production personnel within the steel industry to have contact with. First of all one thinks of various types of suppliers and as such equipment suppliers. A number of customer contacts should also be included in their work. This means that engineers should have substantial cooperation with the marketing department at their own corporation. As a way of keeping abreast of new developments continual contacts with various types of trade and research organizations should be maintained.

These types of contacts are also common contact forms for the surveyed engineers in the production field, (see Figure 5:6). There are three types of corporations which clearly emerge, as being most important. Contacts with equipment suppliers, other steel corporations and customers are clearly considered by many of the engineers as having a direct influence on the results of their work.

On the other hand, contacts with trade and research organizations are considered to be more peripheral. Few of the engineers have designated these organizations as being important in respect

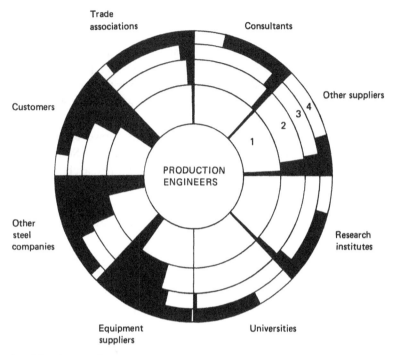

Level 1 = the most important contact partner
Level 2 = one of the two most important contact partners
Level 3 = one of the three most important contact partners
Level 4 = have established contact
(Shadowed areas indicate degree of established contact.)

Figure 5:6 The Contact Network of the Production Engineers.

to the results of their labour. Below we will give a closer description of contacts with those organizations which the majority of
engineers felt were the most important from a contact perspective.

Customer contacts

Ten of the 33 production engineers considered customers to be
the most important contact partners in technical matters. Two of
these 10 engineers have emphasized that in respect to their
response this was a question of foreign customers, while the
remaining engineers included both Swedish and foreign customer
corporations in their response. Most often discussions are conducted with the customer's production personnel.

198

Most contacts are with a single personnel category, while three of the engineers in this group have wider contact networks with the customer corporations. All of these three have contacts with production as well as quality control personnel. One of the engineers also has contacts with the customer's purchasing department. These three engineers also have wide internal contact networks which include many different functions.

There are a number of differences between those three above described engineers who contact several categories of employees at the customer corporations and those who contact one single personnel category. For example, there are two engineers who only communicate with production personnel. These two have compararatively fewer contacts with internal departments and also have a broader background than those engineers described earlier. One of them has worked in several different areas within the same corporation while the other has earlier worked in research both within the steel and motor vehicle industry as well as with marketing in his present corporation.

Relatively few of the engineers have contacts with purchasing personnel in the customer corporations. There are only two engineers who, over and above their contacts with the technological department, also have contacts with the purchasing department. One of these two has, quite uncommonly, earlier worked in purchasing.

Equipment supplier contacts

One fourth, or 8 engineers working in special steel production departments, consider contacts with equipment suppliers to be of the greatest importance to their work. All of these engineers except one have contact with sales personnel. Most of these engineers also hold talks with production personnel as well as with other technicians. One of the engineers only has contact with the equipment suppliers' corporate management. This engineer, compared with the others, makes contact much less commonly. He has contact with these people approximately every other month; while the others most often have contact and even personal meetings with suppliers one or more times a week.

All of the 8 engineers have a wide internal contact network in which many functions are included. Most commonly this includes contact with other production personnel as well as with personnel within marketing, administration, designing and corporate management.

Half of these engineers have, during the entirety of their careers, worked for the same corporation. Among the remaining four engineers two of them have earlier worked in research institutes while the other two have worked at other steel corporations. This appears, however, not to have affected the contact structure. One detail can be mentioned. Two engineers who have worked as production directors meet representatives for the suppliers more often than the others. Both of these engineers have been internally recruited and have a long background in one company. They also have experience in many more areas than the others.

Steel corporation contacts

Contacts between the different steel corporations appear to be common. This does not only include engineers involved in production. The same can be said for the corporate managers. These contacts are most likely a network result. The Swedish steel companies together form a kind of community where more or less everybody above a certain level in the companies know each other.

Approximately one fourth, or 9 of the engineers in the production field, consider steel corporations to be the most important contact partners. It is likely that contacts with these corporations most often occur in the form of exchanges of knowledge and/or experience from, for example, production processes. This is supported by the fact that the engineers almost always communicate with production personnel at the other steel corporations. The engineers, for the most part, only contact people in this personnel category. There is, however, one engineer who has indicated that he, besides production personnel, also has contact with other types of technicians.

Production engineers - a summing up

Engineers in the special steel industry's production divisions are similar, in terms of experience, to the engineers in research. They have worked relatively long periods at their present corporation, though, not equally as long as engineers in research. Even among engineers in production, many have been loyal to the same corporation during the entirety of their careers. Those who have worked for other companies have, as is the case with researchers, for the most part kept within the steel industry. There are, however, examples of employment in other industrial fields, in which case these have been related fields such as mechanical engineering.

In respect to the engineers in production there are three types of corporations which dominate in the choice of the most important contact partner. These are the customer, equipment suppliers and other steel corporations.

In the same way, as was earlier seen in respect to engineers working in research, contacts backwards in the production chain do not occur with personnel from the same type of function. These contacts are conducted with other types of technicians as well as with sales personnel.

On the other hand, contacts directed sideways with, for example, other steel corporations, most likely occur between the same divisions and occupations. We witnessed earlier that engineers working in research contacted exclusively researchers at sideways organisations and here we have seen that production personnel almost only contact production personnel at other steel companies.

Even in respect to forward contacts with customers there are great similarities between engineers in production and research. These contacts most often are conducted between personnel from the same type of occupation; engineers in special steel corporations communicate with the customer's production personnel while engineers working in research communicate with researchers in the customer corporation.

Metallurgical Engineers Working in Marketing

It is of great importance to a corporation's continued technical development to maintain and develop contacts with real and potential customers. The ongoing daily contacts are an important part of this task. Marketing and sales functions within the special steel corporation must as a consequence be handled by personnel who are knowledgeable in technology. This experience can be obtained in different ways, for example, through practical experience and/or some type of technical education.

We found that 19 metallurgical engineers work in the special steel corporation's marketing and sales functions. Approximately one third of these engineers have always worked in the same company. The remaining persons have earlier held employment at one or more external corporations.

In three cases these people were directly recruited from an external manager position. In the other cases recruitment was conducted internally. Of the 16 engineers working in marketing who were recruited internally, half of them have held a different position within the department. The other half came from the corporation's production departments and in two cases from a managerial post.

This most common method of career advancement for these marketing engineers has meant that one can move from one position to another. After having worked in a research division or a research institute and afterwards in various production departments these engineers have gone over to their present position. Sometimes their present management position in marketing is preceeded by a corporate leader position. With only one exception the 19 engineers are, at the lowest, marketing division managers. The exception worked as a sales engineer.

Contact networks

It is something of a platitude that employees in a corporation's marketing and sales functions have rich and important contact exchange with the corporation's customers. Is this also true for engineers or do they have other priorities?

In Figure 5:7 the total technological contact structure for the marketing engineers is shown; here the expected dominance of contacts with customers is illustrated. Contacts with other steel corporations are also very important. It is difficult to say if these contacts are maintained because the steel corporations make purchases from each other or if they occur as a means of exchanging experience. Marketing engineers, as the only vocational category, have in equal degrees contacts with administrative as well as technical personnel in the surrounding organizations.

Approximately half of the 19 marketing engineers have contacts with various research organizations, primarily with differ-

Level 1 = the most important contact partner
Level 2 = one of the two most important contact partners
Level 3 = one of the three most important contact partners
Level 4 = have established contact
(Shadowed areas indicate degree of established contact.)

Figure 5:7 The Contact Network of the Marketing Personnel.

ent trade associations. These contacts are most likely maintained so that engineers can have an opportunity to view the industry's development in the various production fields. There are many engineers who have these types of contacts: only a few consider that they are of importance in their daily work.

Contact with customers

The most dense section in Figure 5:7 represents the engineer's customer contacts. Twelve of 19 marketing engineers consider these contacts to be important. In ten cases they were the most important external contacts they maintained. Almost half of these engineers have always worked in their present steel corporation.

All of the engineers working in marketing have in principal identical backgrounds. Regardless of whether they have always worked in their present company or not, their career histories are similar. After having worked ten to fifteen years in various research and production departments, they have gone over to marketing. In some cases they have first held a lower position, before securing a management post.

In respect to these similarities in experience it is not surprising that their contact networks have nearly the same structure - overall the marketing engineer's contact network with the customer is relatively small. They most often contact the customer corporation's buyer and in a few cases production personnel as well as other technicians.

A marketing manager can be said to have a somewhat wider contact network where contacts with research and customer's corporate management are included. This engineer's internal contact network is similar to the others. Internally, contact exchange occurs for the most part upward and horizontally within the corporation's organization.

Contacts with other steel corporations

We have earlier seen that many engineers in marketing, over and above their customer contacts, also have contacts with representatives from other steel corporations. Six of the 14 engineers who contact steel corporations consider these companies to be the most important external contact partner. Compared with those who consider the customer to be the most important, the greatest difference is which person the marketing engineers get into contact with. In respect to the customers the contacts are with buyers. In the steel corporations, on the other hand, the contacts are almost exclusively with representatives from production.

We can only speculate about the reasons for this difference. The most possible one is that the engineers use their contact network in order to follow the technical development of their competitors. Another possible explanation is that these six engineers are involved in cooperation projects with other steel corporations.

Otherwise, no large differences can be found among the engineers in marketing functions. We can see that they comprise the most consistent group we have studied. Both their background in respect to their career progress and the structure of their contact network are, for the most part, the same for all of the marketing engineers. By moving from one position to another and as such gaining experience in various corporations these engineers have received a multi-dimensional competence. They have understood how to utilize these possibilities by moving up in their careers. This has consequently, after a 10 to 15 year involvement in the industry, helped these men, in many cases, into high management positions in the Swedish special steel industry.

Metallurgical Engineers and the Network

In conclusions we wish to comment on three different issues. Firstly, the perceptions of the most important external partners in technical questions will be summarized. Secondly we wish to comment on the variation between the background and position of the individual and their contact networks. Thirdly, a more complete picture of the engineers' relationship to the special steel network will be given.

Important external organizations

The total picture is given in Table 5:2. Customers are perceived to be the most important by 38%, other steel companies by 20% and equipment suppliers by 14% of those surveyed. However, there is a certain difference between the four vocational groups.

Customers are perceived to be the most important by all four groups but of especially high value to corporate managers and marketing executives. Other steel companies are very much appreciated by production engineers and marketing personnel but not at all to the same extent by corporate management and R&D engineers. Equipment suppliers, on the other hand, are highly valued by R&D and production engineers but received no votes at all from managers and marketing personnel. Research units are mainly mentioned by R&D engineers and consultants are most appreciated by corporate managers.

The total figures show that engineers judge that there are important development organizations all around the steel compan-

Table 5:2   Most Important External Organization in regard to Technical Development.

	Total	Corporate managers	R&D	Production	Marketing
Customers	38%	62%	26%	30%	53%
Steel corporations	20%	12%	10%	27%	32%
Equipment supplier	14%	0%	19%	24%	0%
Research units	6%	0%	16%	3%	0%
Branch org.	4%	0%	3%	3%	11%
Consultants	4%	12%	3%	3%	0%
Other suppliers	3%	0%	3%	6%	0%
Don't know	10%	12%	19%	3%	5%
	99%	98%	99%	99%	101%
Number	99	16	31	33	19

ies. Forward there are the customers, to the sides there are other steel companies and trade associations, and backwards there are different types of suppliers, consultants and research units. However, how much these different categories of external organizarions are appreciated and looked upon as important is very much dependent on the position of the person judging.

Heterogeneity of contact networks

In this chapter we have investigated the contact network of a rather homogeneous group. They have the same education and they work in the same type of company. Despite this the dominant result can be summarized in the word heterogeneity at least on the individual level. The contact networks seem to be very individualized even when measured on an aggregated level, as has been done here. Different careers, interests and backgrounds in terms other than education is enough to create this heterogeneity. This result indicates the importance of organizing - of making the right personnel combinations - in order to create overview and good utilization of external units.

This heterogeneity on the individual level, however, seems to create a certain homogeneity on the network level. The contacts, the changes between positions, etc., all take place within a rather narrow number of companies, creating a very well structured network which probably functions well 'internally' but experiences certain difficulties in absorbing new ideas.

Networking

It is possible to identify two completely different ways of operating in the network. First, there are those in high positions who in principle are stationary in the network. These engineers make their careers in one and the same corporation. On the other hand we have the more mobile engineer who moves about between different corporations in the network. These two main types are not defined wholly by their vocational positions; both types are represented in all of the surveyed vocational groups.

It appears, however, that there are, depending on the vocational group, small variations in distribution between these two categories. Remaining are the loyal engineers in all four vocational groups; we have found that there are more 'loyal' employees in research and production than in the other vocational groups.

There are also a number of groupings in the two main categories, the loyal engineers and the more mobile employees. Within the loyal group we have found engineers who have worked almost all their working lives in the same position while others have changed from position to position within the corporation. It has been seen that there are a number of marked differences between these different groups. Those engineers working in research who have, during the entirety of their careers worked for the same corporation, have often worked exclusively in research functions. On the other hand, all of the more mobile employees in corporate management have moved from position to position within the company.

In the same way we can identify two different variants of the mobile employee. One group of mobile employees have moved from industry to industry while another group have moved from corporation to corporation within the steel industry. A good example of this first group are certain of the engineers in marketing. These engineers have often worked in other industries. Also, these engineers often have experience in different types of functions such as research and production. The researchers are, on the other hand, in certain cases representatives of the second group of mobile employees. These engineers have, in a number of cases, moved from one corporation to another, but this has almost always been within the steel industry. Another characteristic of these engineers is that they have had the same type of work tasks despite the fact that they have moved from one company to another.

In conclusion we can consequently, in these two categories of mobile employee, isolate two sub-groups dependent on whether the engineer has worked in one or in several areas. We can, for example, in the group working in marketing, find engineers who have worked within different industries and in different areas. Another case, which in our study was not as common as the previous one, is a group who have worked in various industries but with the same type of work task. Some few cases of this can be found among engineers working in research.

In the same way we can see that there are two sub-groups among the mobile employees who have moved from one company to another within the steel industry. Among the corporate management engineers there are some good examples of a category of mobile employee who has been involved in many different functions. Secondly, there are mobile employees who have moved from one steel company to another but have during the entirety of their careers worked in the same area. Several examples of this can be found among the engineers working in research.

How do these mobile employees function in the network? Some systematic differences have been presented in this study. Firstly, there are those who have been 'forced' into temporary mobilization because of pressure from the network. The basis of this statement can be found for the most part in the observation made of engineers working in research. In order to obtain certain positions it appears that there is an understood demand from the corporations in the network that experience be gained from at least one other steel corporation's research department.

Secondly, there are mobile employees who utilize the network systematically; this person can be called an 'opportunist'. A common example of conscious mobility in order to forward one's career has been observed in certain corporate leaders and marketing personnel. These engineers have often begun their careers with research positions after which they transferred to various production departments so as to in time attain their current position. These changes have occurred between various corporations and between various industries. Most of these engineers have worked for different steel companies and many have earlier held positions in customer and/or supplier companies.

Quite naturally, these two main types of engineers have different roles to play in the corporation. Those who, during the entirety of their careers, have been loyal to one and the same corporation have clearly a profound knowledge of that corporation. They have had the possibility of building up an extensive internal contact network. They can be said to function as a coordinator of the internal flow of information. Most likely they do not have an equally as broad external contact network. Their foremost function is to operate within their own corporation. The mobile employee has, on the other hand, a completely different role. Through his movement among different corporations this type of engineer has been able to obtain a wide external contact network. This contact network has most likely been carried over to the present company. Because of this it can be expected that this employee functions as a channel between the corporation and its external environment.

Notes to Chapter 5

1. The judgement of if an event should be considered as special or not can in the light of what is happening afterwards be changed; this can be compared with the enactment process described by Weick (1969, p. 63ff).

2. The term strategic windows has been used in the business policy literature to characterize this phenomenon.

3. For an exellent discussion of the connection between the individual, his association with different groups and his profession, see Scott (1982, p. 137f and 222f).

4. The general connection between the individual's position within a network and corresponding opportunities and power is discussed among others in Cook & Emerson (1978) and Granovetter (1973).

5. This can be compared with for example the existence of interlocked directorates, see Pfeffer & Salancik (1978).

6. the toal population was 587 individuals. The response rate was 73% (within the group working within the special steel industry it was 85%). The data collection was done through a postal enquiry which means that the questions were highly standardized.

Chapter Six

STRATEGIC IMPLICATIONS

The network approach seems to be a natural choice for managers. This is not at all surprising; social networks have been used for thousands of years in order to increase power or to get things done[1]. Our network concepts have been developed from an empirical base - i.e. we have identified networks from reality and not from theory. We have met many managers who have been very skilled in their way of handling networks as a result of experience of a life-time spent in networks. As a consequence we will avoid giving detailed advice regarding the practical handling of networks. Instead, we believe that we can be of much more help by identifying and discussing more general network issues. Thus our contribution is rather to integrate known details to a more comprehensive body of knowledge.

Our implications can at a first glance look trivial but are basically quite the opposite. Compare our implications with the recommendations found in the management literature and you will find large differences. The business world that we describe is quite different - it is a world that is more structured in some respects but paradoxically less structured in other respects than the world described in the standard text books. Ours is more structured because the networks give more specific limitations than the traditional market concepts. It is less structured as everything is possible to an actor who can mobilize others; in other words there is no invisible rule/law that forces the network into some specific state, as is assumed in the market theory. It is a world where one actor can do very little by himself but if a sufficient number of other actors are mobilized everything is possible[2].

This duality can be explained by the fact that the network is a product of interaction, it is interacted. The network is the framework within which the interaction takes place but it is also the result of the interaction. Thus, it is affected by the exchanges between the actors.

There have been specific implication comments given in the previous chapters. These will not be repeated here. Instead the

210

discussion will be centered around four general issues which are believed to be critical in the handling of networks. These are;
  –the importance of getting involved
  –the importance of having power of endurance
  –the importance of having both strong and weak ties
  –the importance of being able to defend and change positions
These four issues will be dealt with both in general terms and in relation to technical development.

The Importance of Getting Involved

The network is formed through interactions and relates, as we have described earlier, actors, activities and resources to each other. In doing so it also constitutes the base for the technical, social, and economic/institutional structure. The technical structure consists of specific dependencies between activities within and between activity cycles. Another type of technical dependency exists between activities and resources. The social structure can be identified in terms of language, morale, perceptions and expectations. The economic/institutional structure can be identified in terms of ownership, share holding, interlocked directorates, contracts, etc. These structures, because they normally do not completely overlap create an awarness and a tension around the positions of the actors viz a viz each other.

The only way to get into an interacted network is by interaction with already established actors. Futhermore the only way to learn how a network functions in a more detailed way is by interaction. By approaching some of the actors others will feel threatened and react in different ways. Thus, there are always problems associated with getting into a network. There must be good reasons given to the others in order to convince them to establish a new relationship. Some type of 'entrance fee' has to be paid.

This fee must be related to the activities and/or resources controlled by the other actors as these are the attributes characterizing the actor according to the network approach. In other words the actor must control some activity or resource that is of interest to the other actors. The activity, or activities, can be of a competitive (can be used instead) or complementary (can be used

211

together) nature. The resource can in the same way be either complementary or competitive. It can be a physical, knowledge, or demand resource. The resources can be controlled directly by the actor or indirectly through relationships. The critical issue is that the activity or resource is of interest to some of the actors within the network; so interesting in fact that they are prepared to make the necessary changes.

Usually, the value of an activity or a resource is increased if it is adapted in some way. Here, technical development can be of great help and is probably a necessary requirement in most situations. The technical development can be in the form of product development but even more common are changes in the production process. As we have described earlier transformation activities are parts of activity cycles which also include transaction activities. When changing the latter the former must be adapted. Technical development is in this way of significant importance when approaching a new network.

In approaching a network two distinctly different methods can be used. One is to start at the 'periphery' and successively - step by step - try to force oneself towards the centre. The alternative way is to identify a centrally located actor and try to use an 'inoculation strategy'. This means establishing a close relationship with this key actor in order to later on use his position as a base for further activities. Both ways are time-consuming but the first to a higher degree. The second can be faster but it is at the same time more risky. Everything is in this case built upon just one relationship. If this relationship is broken everything is lost. This is the main reason why this strategy often is combined with institutional control (ownership, merger, etc). However, as many companies have learnt the hard way, institutional control does not automatically give access to the coveted position[3].

The pattern of technical development is quite different in the two alternatives. In the inoculation case all technical activities are mainly directed towards the establishment of the basic relationship. One fruitful way can be to do this in a cooperative project together with the counterpart. In the 'periphery' case technical development has to be of a step-wise character, successively adopting the company to many different counterparts.

Which of the above two strategies is chosen depends to a

large extent on the existing opportunities. This indicates the importance of timing - i.e. to do the right thing at the right moment. As we have shown earlier in this book the connections between activities and resources can vary over time. The network thus opens up during certain time periods due to changes in the combination of activities and resources. The opportunities of entering into a network thus varies over time and is consequently an important strategic issue. It is not only important when choosing between the alternative strategies but also during the time period when the strategy is put into action.

Power of Endurance

The network gives both restrictions and possibilities. It is interacted which means that nobody can change anything by himself; however, through successful interaction anything is possible. Thus, in order to make changes others must be mobilized. This is usually a process that is both time consuming and seldom straightforward or simple.

The technical development process is not a simple one from a knowledge point of view. Instead it is often a matter of trial and error. Technical solutions do not always function as planned, and new ways must often be found in order to go ahead.

Both the mobilization and the technical development processes are usually interwoven in product or process developments, and as a result power of endurance becomes a critical factor. Many companies have realized this. As one manager put it:

> *We less and less judge the idea - the innovation. Instead we more and more judge the individual that will have the responsibility to see it through.*

One reason for the importance of having power of endurance is that the development processes are so tightly connected to the time factor. This has several consequences. Firstly, there is a need to see the individual technical development process, its bases and effects, as a part of a much larger and longer process. This is important when choosing between different potential projects as well as when evaluating the results of an on-going or completed project. Thus each project must be put into a larger time perspective. Secondly, the actor must be able to get the time factor working for him. It can be done through relating his own process to other processes that are at hand in the network. These other processes can be not only of a technical but also of a structural, economic or social character. Thirdly, and related to the previous consequence, individual processes must be adaptable as the circumstances are changing over time.

There are several means that can be used in order to increase a company's power of endurance. Three major ones will be commented upon here.

The first means is cooperation in different forms. It can be with other actors in individual projects. Such cooperation increases both the available resources and the mobilization possibilities. However, it can also create problems, as has been discussed earlier. Another more indirect form of cooperation is when a certain project is coordinated with other change processes, in order to become a part of a larger process. In this case the in-house development activities must be coordinated with development work carried out by others. Both these two types of cooperation have been illustrated in a number of cases throughout this book.

The second means regards the organizational climate, which in good cases can support and in bad cases deteriorate the power of endurance. One positive feature can be that the organization directs its members towards small wins (Weick 1984, p. 41). The concept of small wins emphasizes the importance of dividing large problems and large projects into smaller less overwhelming sections. It is in this way action oriented and closely related to expressions such as 'get into the mud' and 'get through the mud' used earlier in this book. Furthermore it points to the necessity of also rewarding small improvements as well as to the need of securing quality in the details.

One common way to try to create the 'right' climate has been to separate larger projects into special organizational units (Littler, 1984). This can certainly have some positive effects but also some serious drawbacks. It decreases the integration with the rest of the company in such a way that the project might not become part of a larger whole, the importance of which we have stressed earlier. This decreases the possibilities of using some of the results (spin-offs) as well as making it more difficult to give continuous inputs from different company functions. Thus, our main recommendation is to keep project groups integrated within the organization as long as possible and remove them when it can be shown that they have features that are quite different from the rest of the organization.

A third means that can be used in order to 'wait for' the right moment is to 'mummify'. This is an alternative that can be chosen instead of cancelling a project. In situations when all opportunities have been tried and everything seems to be blocked, but where there is still some hope that it might change later on, one alternative can be to try to preserve the project - to mummify it - until the changes occur. Time must pass, and during that period a minimum of resources should be spent; it must be possible, however, to restart the project quickly and easily when the right moment comes.

The Importance of Strong and Weak Ties

In a convincing article Granovetter (1973) stresses the importance of weak ties. Granovetter uses a simple triad in order to show that innovations must be spread between groups through weak ties or as he puts it: 'no strong tie is a bridge'. This is probably a very important function of weak ties, i.e. that they are used as communication channels. In this book we have on the other hand stressed the importance of strong ties - close relationships - as a means of mobilizing external resources for the company's technical development. Thus, there seems to be need for both strong and weak ties.

The function of strong ties is to get external resources coordinated with the company's resources. This gives the company increased strength. Close relationships require large investments and, as a consequence, the company can only have a few of them. They create possibilities of developing knowledge, of taking larger risks, and so on. In this way they increase the size of the company, which becomes part of a larger whole. Close relationships also create possibilities of developing products together, which can be seen as an example of how relationships are a prerequisite for the use of each others' resources in a more extensive way.

The function of weak ties is the opposite and in this way complementary. Firstly the company can have a large number of weak ties. They do not demand as large resources as the strong ties do. They are mostly used in order to receive information from different areas. With the help of weak ties the company can cover very large areas without making large investments. The company does not need to have direct contacts with everyone; instead it can trust some strategically chosen nodes. Another important function of weak ties is that they are potential strong ties. In the muddling through process one never knows when some specific competence is needed. When such a need arises all the weak ties become potential alternatives.

In total all the strong and weak ties compose the company set (Evan, 1966). This set varies over time and needs to be analyzed now and then. Do we have a sufficient number of strong ties? Do we have too few weak ties? Do we have weak ties within new and interesting technological areas? etc.

In the analysis of the company set, one should not forget to look carefully at the old relationships. Usually too much interest is devoted to the new relationships ('new friends') as these are perceived to be more exciting. It is also too easy to believe that the future profit lies in new things and not in old ones. Old relationships are seldom fully utilized and there are always possibilities for taking advantage of 'new' sides of old friends. Furthermore, profitable new products or production processes are very often developed from the base of earlier products or processes. All together this shows the importance of analysing and developing the established set of relationships. This could also be described as the need to use stability in order to be able to create changes (see Chapter 1).

The ties are handled by people. As shown in Chapter 5 it is individuals who have the contacts. Thus, it is very important for the company to

–recruit personnel with certain contacts (personal networks)
–influence the personnel to establish or develop certain contacts with others

216

–circulate the personnel in order to combine the different individual contact networks with each other

– 'export' people to other actors in order to facilitate contacts with those actors.

Positions and the Roles of the Company

Each actor combines certain activities with certain resources in the interaction with certain other actors and is in this way always unique. The identity of the company can be seen as this interlocking of activities, resources and actors. This identity can also be described in terms of a position within a certain network. But as the company belongs to several networks it will have several positions. All companies described in relation to a specific network in this book are also actors in other networks. These networks can be identified in relation to raw materials ('the iron ore network', 'the wood network', etc) to technologies (e.g. 'the hydraulic network',) to customers ('the automotive network) to geographical areas ('the U.K. network') and to institutional/financial units ('the Wallenberg network'). Consequently a company has a whole number of positions. As an effect it will be perceived quite differently from varying angles and this is furthermore one prerequisite for efficiency and ability to survive according to the network approach. A company can in this way be compared to a theatre actor. A good actor should be able to play very different roles. However, a large difference is that the company has to play all the roles at the same time. It is impossible, of course, to play all the roles perfectly but, fortunately, all the roles are not equally important. Some are more critical and will be dominant. But all the others must receive a certain minimum of attention as to avoid becoming serious liabilities. Thus, in a network, attributes such as heterogeneity, inconsistency, and adaptability are more important than their opposites.

All positions are interacted - i.e. the result of interaction processes - and they are related to each other in a complex and multifarious way. Positions can also be created by individual companies which succeed in 'building' new networks. One such case in Sweden is IKEA, the furniture manufacturer, which succeeded in (or was forced into) building up a unique supplier network (Kinch, 1984).

The combination of positions gives the company a complicated set of roles to play. Earlier interactions create the framework. In the very short run this framework is usually very restrictive but through interaction it can be changed. Some of the roles are complementary and are in this way able to be integrated with one another while others are and even should be contradictory. The networks and their development are so complex and impossible to predict that the company has to live with contradictions. There is in this sense no reason to design one 'super role' and judge all activities, positions or roles in respect to such.

A role can be played in a lot of different ways. The position creates the base but then it is up to the actor to do the acting. Basically this acting can be oriented either towards defending the earlier position or towards changing it. In both cases there are an uncountable number of ways to do this.

Technological development is an important tool in this role playing. It can be used - in most situations even must be used - both when defending positions and in order to change them. The protection of a position means that technological development within the role playing is directed towards a stabilization of existing activity cycles and/or the use of some resources. This includes real capital investments, day-to-day rationalizations and marginal product improvements. In order to increase the stabilization effects large and important counterparts should be approached in order to make complementary changes in a cooperative way.

In situations where the intention is to try to change the position, technological development must be used in order to break the established interlocking of activities, resources, and counterparts. This usually brings changes in both transformation and transaction activities indicating in turn both process and product developments.

We concluded earlier that a company has several positions. Therefore, the normal case is that the company, in its role playings, must combine the defence of certain positions with the change of others. Together this creates rather complicated demands on technical development. Furthermore, technical development is in itself complicated because it includes a large number of different activities such as day-to-day rationalizations, capital investments, and new product developments. Thus, technical development is a key element in networking, it is however, by no means a simple instrument. The technical development strategy must reflect this complexity. A good strategy may, against this background, be characterized by ambiguity rather than clarity, by contradictions and conflicts rather than conformity, and by action rather than planning.

Notes to Chapter 6

1. Belshaw (1965) has shown how social networks have been used in very old societies.

2. This can also be described as getting other companies to develop in the same direction as one's own company. Basically this is the same problem as the internal organization faces when trying to integrate and direct the personnel. Theoretical models and concepts developed within organizational theory should therefore also be of value when analysing this kind of 'external' problems.

3. The formal take over of a company does not automatically lead to a real take over in terms of total control of activities or relationships. To get this control takes time and needs investments. If the company taking over tries to hurry up the process too much there is a danger that important relationships will get destroyed.

REFERENCES

Aldrich, H.E., 1979, *Organizations and Environments*, Englewood Cliffs, N.J.; Prentice-Hall.

Aldrich, H., Whetten, D.A., 1981, Organization-sets, Action-sets, and Networks: Making the most of Simplicity, in Nyström. P.C., and W.H., Starbuck (eds.) *Handbook of Organizational Design*, Vol. 1, pp. 385-408, Oxford University Press.

Allen, T. J., 1977, *Managing the Flow of Technology*, Boston, Mass: MIT Press.

Axelsson, B., 1983, Teknisk utveckling i köpar-säljarrelationer. 14 storförbrukares bild av de svenska specialstålföretagens roll och betydelse. (Technological Developments in Buyer-Seller Relationships. 14 Significant Users View of the Swedish Special Steel Companies Role and Importance). *Working Paper 1983/6, Department of Business Administration, University of Uppsala.*

Axelsson, B., Håkansson, H., 1979, *Wikmanshyttans uppgång och fall. En analys av ett stålföretag och dess omgivning under 75 år.* (The Rise and Fall of Wikmanshyttan. An Analysis of a Steel Company and its Environment during 75 years), Lund: Studentlitteratur.

Axelsson, B., Håkansson, H., 1984, *Inköp för konkurrenskraft.* (Purchasing for Competitive Power), Stockholm: Liber.

Axelsson, H., Lövgren, L., 1984, Externa relationers betydelse för producentvaruföretagets tekniska utveckling - Block Tool System, En fallstudie. (The Importance of External Relationships for the Technical Development of a Producer Company. - The Block Tools System. A Case study), *C-report, Department of Business Administration, University of Uppsala.*

Baker, M. J., (ed.) 1979, *Industrial Innovation. Technology, Policy, Diffusion,* London: Macmillan Press.

Baranson, J., 1978, *Technology and the Multinationals*, Massachusetts, Toronto: Lexington Books.

Belshaw, C.S., 1965, *Traditional Exchange and Modern Markets*, Englewood Cliffs, N.J.: Prentice Hall.

Bengtsson, W., 1983, ASEA i bergshanteringens tjänst (ASEA in the Service of the Mining Industry). In: *Teknik i ASEA* (Technology in ASEA), Västerås: ASEA AB.

Bergqvist, S., Hamfelt, C., Lindberg, A-C., 1983, Specialstålindustrins ledande personal. (The Managers of the Special Steel Industry), *C-report, Department of Business Administration, University of Uppsala.*

Björk. L., Edwall, Å., 1982, Teknisk utveckling och marknadsföring inom borrstålsområdet (Technical Development and Marketing of Drill Steel) *C-report, Department of Business Administration University of Uppsala.*

Blau, P.M., 1964, *Exchange and Power in Social Life*, New York: John Wiley.

Blois, K.J., 1984, Developments in Production Technologies and their Implications for Marketing Management, Paper presented at the *International Research Seminar on Industrial Marketing, August 29-31, 1984, at the Stockholm School of Economics.*

Brunsson. N., 1982, The Irrationality of Action and Action Rationality; Decisions, Ideologies and Organizational Actions, *Journal of Management Studies,* Vol. 19, No. 1, pp. 29-44.

Carlson, S., 1970, Some Notes on the Dynamics of International Economic Integration, *Swedish Journal of Economics,* Vol. 72, No. 1, pp. 21-39.

Carlsson, B., Dahmén, E., Grufman, A., Josepsson, M., Örtengren, J., 1979, *Teknik och industristruktur - 70-talets ekonomiska kris i historisk belysning*

(Technology and Industry Structure - the Crisis of the 70s in the Light of History), Stockholm: IUI, IVA.

Cook, K.S., Emerson, R.M., 1978, Power, Equity and Commitment in Exchange Networks, *American Sociological Review*, Vol. 43, October, pp. 721-39.

Cunningham, M.T., and Kettlewood, K., 1976, Source Loyalty in Freight Transport Buying, *European Journal of Marketing*, Vol. 10, No. 1, pp. 60-79.

Cunningham & Turnbull., 1982, Inter-Organizational Personal Contact Patterns, in Håkansson, H., (ed.), *International Marketing and Purchasing of Industrial Goods*, Chichester: John Wiley.

Czepiel, J.A., 1974, Word-of-Month Processes in the Diffusion of Major Technological Innovation, *Journal of Marketing Research*, Vol. 11, May, pp. 172-80.

Dahl, R.A., 1957, The Concept of Power. *Behavioural Science*, Vol. 2, No. 3, pp. 201-15.

Epstein, E.M., 1969, *The Corporation in American Politics*. Englewood Cliffs, N.J.: Prentice Hall.

Evan, W.M., 1966, The Organization - Set: Toward a Theory of Interorganizational Relations, in Thompson, J., (ed.), *Approaches to Organizational Design*, Pittsburg: University of Pittsburg Press.

Ford, D.I., Håkansson, H., Johanson, J., 1985, How Do Companies Interact? Paper presented at the *2nd Open IMP-Research Seminarium on International Marketing, University of Uppsala 1985*.

Galbraith, J.K., 1952, *American Capitalism: The Concept of Countervailing Power*, Boston: Houghton Mifflin.

Glete, J., 1984, High Technology and Industrial Networks. Some Notes on the Cooperation Between Swedish High Technology Industries and their Customers. Paper presented at the *International Research Seminar on Industial Marketing, August 29-31, 1984 at the Stockholm School of Economics.*

Gold, B., 1979, Inter-Industry Repercursions of Major Technological Innovations, in Baker, M., (ed.) *Industrial Innovation. Technology, Policy, Diffusion.* London: Macmillan Press.

Golding, I., 1983, New Product Development: A Literature Review, *European Journal of Marketing*, Vol. 17, No. 3, pp. 3-30.

Granovetter, M.S., 1973, The Strength of Weak Ties, *American Journal of Sociology*, Vol. 78, No. 6, pp. 1360-80.

Goldman, K., 1978, *Det industriella systemet* (The Industrial System) Stockholm: Bonniers.

Hägg, I., Johanson, J., (eds.), 1982, *Företag i nätverk - ny syn på konkurrenskraft* (Firms in Networks - a new Perspective of Competitive Power), Stockholm: SNS.

Håkansson, H., 1979, Marknadsföring av specialstål (Marketing of Special Steel), *Research Report 1979/2, Department of Business Administration, University of Uppsala.*

Håkansson, H., (ed.), 1982, *International Marketing and Purchasing of Industrial Goods. An Interaction Approach*, Chichester: John Wiley.

Håkansson, H., 1982, *Teknisk utveckling och marknadsföring* (MTC 19), (Technical Development and Marketing), Stockholm: Liber.

Håkansson, H., Johanson, J., 1984, A Model of Industrial Networks, *Working paper, Department of Business Administation, University of Uppsala.*

Håkansson, H., Laage-Hellman, J., 1984, Developing a Network R&D Strategy, *Journal of Product Innovation Management*, Vol. 1, No. 4, p. 224ff.

Håkansson, H., Laage-Hellman, J., Axelsson, B., 1983, Ramprogram för kunskapsutveckling - utvärdering av industriell förankring (Research Programs for Knowledge Development -Assessment of Industrial Liasions), *STU-rapport*

82-5372, *Stockholm:* The National Board for Technical Development.

Hallén, L., 1985, A Comparision of Strategic Marketing Approaches, in Turnbull, P.W., Valla, J-P., (eds.), *Strategies for International Industrial Marketing*, London: Croom Helm (in print).

Hammarkvist, K-O., Håkansson, H., Mattsson, L-G., 1982, *Marknadsföring för konkurrenskraft* (Marketing for Competive Power), Malmö: Liber.

Hedberg, B., 1979, How Organizations Learn and Unlearn, in Nyström, P., Starbuck, W., (eds.), *Handbook of Organizational Design*, Vol. 1, pp. 3-27, Oxford University Press.

Hirschman, A.O., 1970, *Exit, Voice and Loyalty*, Cambridge, Mass.: Harvard University Press.

Johanson, J., Wiedersheim-Paul, F., 1975, The Internationalization of the Firm - Four Swedish Case Studies, *Journal of Management Studies*, Vol. 2, No. 3, pp. 305-22.

Johanson, J., Mattsson, L-G., 1984, Marketing Investments and Market Investments in Industrial Networks, Paper presented at the *International Research Seminar on Industrial Marketing, Stockholm School of Economics 1984.*

Kennedy. A.M., 1983, The Adoption and Diffusion of New Industrial Products: A Literature Review, *European Journal of Marketing*, Vol. 17, No. 3, pp. 31-88.

Kinch, N., 1984, Strategy and Structure of Supplier Relationships in IKEA. A Case from the Furniture and Interior Decoration Industry, in Hägg, I., Wiedersheim-Paul, F., (eds.), *Between Market and Hierarchy*, Department of Business Administration, University of Uppsala.

Kostiainen, T., 1984, Teknisk utveckling genom samarbete - en fallstudie av en ny separeringsprocess, (Technical Development through Cooperation - a Case study of a new Separation Technique), *C-report, Department of Business Administration, University of Uppsala.*

Kutschker, M., 1982, Power and Dependence in Industrial Marketing, in Håkansson, H., (ed.), *International Marketing and Purchasing of Industrial Goods, An Interaction Approach*, Chichester: John Wiley.

Laage-Hellman, J., 1984, The Role of External Technical Exchange in R&D. An Empirical Study of the Swedish Special Steel Industry, *MTC Research Report No. 18*, Stockholm: Marknadstekniskt centrum.

Lindblom, C.E., 1959, The Science of Muddling Through, *Public Administration Review*, American Society for Public Administration, Washington D.C., Vol. 19, Spring, pp. 79-88. Also published in Ansoff, I., (ed.) 1969, *Business Strategy. Selected Readings*, pp. 41-60, Harmondsworth: Penguin Education.

Littler, D.A., 1984, Organization and New Product Development, Paper presented at the *International Research Seminar on Industrial Marketing at Stockholm School of Economics. August 29-31, 1984.*

Lundgren, A., 1985, Datoriserad bildbehandling i Sverige, (Computerized Image Processing in Sweden), *Working Paper, EFI. Stockholm School of Economics.*

Mattsson, L-G., 1985, An Application of a Network Approach to Marketing. Defending and Changing Market Positions, in Dholakia, Arndt, J., (eds.), *Alternative Paradigms for Widening Marketing Theory*. Greenwich, Conn: JAI Press (in print).

Menzel, H., 1967, Planning the Consequences of Unplanned Action in Scientific Communication, in De Reuck, A., Knight, J., (eds.), *Communication in Scinece*, London: J & A Churchill.

Ny Teknik, 1983:4, pp. 30-31.

Parkinson, S.T., 1982, The Role of the User in Successful New Product Develop-

222

ment, *R&D Management*, Vol. 12, No. 3, pp. 123-31.

Parkinson, S.T., & Avlonitis, G. J., 1984, The Organisational Adoption Decision Process: A Study of a Major Technological Innovation (FMS), Paper presented at the *International Research Seminar on Industrial Marketing, August 29-31, 1984, at the Stockholm School of Economics.*

Penfield, Jr., P.L., 1982, Small is Big: The Microelectronic Challange, in *The Innovative Process - Evolution vs. Revolution, Proceedings of a symposium for Senior Executives November 12-13 1981, Massachusetts Institute of Technology.*

Pfeffer, J., & Salancik, G.R., 1978, *The External Control of Organizations. A Resource Dependence Perspective.* New York: Harper & Row.

Porter, M.E., 1983, The Technological Dimension of Competitive Strategy, Research on Technological Innovation, *Management and Policy*, Vol. 1, Greenwich, Conn.: JAI Press.

Rogers, E.M., Kincaid, D.L., 1981, *Communication Networks.* Towards a New Paradigm for Research, New York: Free Press.

Rogers, E.M., Larsen, J.K., 1984, *Silicon Valley Fever*, New York: Basic Books.

Sahal, D., 1980, Technological Progress and Policy, in Sahal., (ed.), *Research, Development, and Technological Innovation*, Lexington: Lexington Books.

Scott, R.W., 1982, *Organizations. Rational, Natural, and Open Systems.* Englewood Cliffs, N.J.: Prentice-Hall.

Steindl, J., 1980, Technical Progress and Evolution, in Sahal, D., (ed.), *Research, Development, and Technological Innovation*, Lexington: Lexington Books.

Teubal, M., 1979, On User Needs and Need Determination, Aspects of the Theory of Technological Innovation, in Baker, M., (ed.), *Industrial Innovation. Technology, Policy, Diffusion.* London: Macmillan Press.

Turnbull, P.W., & Valla, J-P., (eds.) 1985, *Strategies for International Industrial Marketing*, London: Croom Helm, (in print).

Utterback, J.M., 1982, The Innovative Process: Evolution vs. Revolution, in: *The Innovative Process: Evolution vs. Revolution, Proceedings of a Symposium for Senior Executives November 12-13 1981, Massachusetts Institute of Technology.*

Utterback, J.M., & Abernathy, W.J., 1975, A Dynamic Model of Process and Product Innovation, *Omega*, Vol. 3, No. 6, pp. 639-56.

Van de Ven, A.H., Emmit, D.G., Koeing, R., 1975, Frameworks for Interorganizational Analysis, in Negandhi, A.R., (ed.), *Interorganizational Theory*, Kent State University Press.

Veckans Affärer (The Business of the Week), No. 25, 1983.

Von Hippel, E., 1977, The Dominant Role of the Users in Semiconductor and Electronic Subassembly Process Innovation, *IEEE Transactions on Engineering Management*, Vol. EM-24, No. 2, pp. 60-71.

Von Hippel, E., 1978, Successful Industrial Products from Customer Ideas, *Journal of Marketing*, Vol. 42, No. 1, pp. 39-49.

Von Hippel, E., 1982, Appropriability of Innovation Benefit as a Predictor of the Source of Innovation, *Research Policy*, Vol. 11, No. 2, pp. 95-115.

Waluszewski, A., 1985, SCA-fallet: Tekniska utvecklingsprocesser inom ett företag (The SCA-case: Technical Development Processes within a Company), *Working paper, Department of Business Administration, University of Uppsala.*

Webster, Jr. F.E., Wind, Y., 1972, *Organizational Buying Behaviour*, Englewood Cliffs, N.J.: Prentice-Hall.

Weick, K.E., 1969, *The Social Psychology of Organizing,* Reading, Mass.:

Addison Wesley (2nd ed. 1979).

Weick, K.E., 1976, Educational Organizations as Loosely Coupled Systems, *Administrative Science Quarterly*, Vol. 21, No. 1, pp. 1-19.

Weick, K.E., 1984, Small Wins, Redefining the Scale of Social Problems. *American Psyshologist*, Vol. 39, No. 1, pp. 40-9.

Williamson, O.E., 1975, *Markets and Hierarchies: Anlysis and Antitrust Implications*, New York, N.Y.: Free Press.

Williamson, O.E., 1979, Transaction-Cost Economics; The Governance of Contractual Relations, *The Journal of Law and Economics*, Vol. 22, No. 2, pp. 232-262.

Wind. Y., 1970, Industrial Source Loyalty, *Journal of Marketing Research*, Vol. VIII, November, pp. 433-6.

SUBJECT INDEX

activity 60-7, 73–7, 107, 211
   chains 15
activity cycles 15, 88, 119, 161, 211
   patterns 138
actors 25, 60–7, 73–7, 97, 107, 125, 211
adaptation 4, 9, 11, 13, 110–1
adoption 125
aircraft engine industry 50, 66
A.K Eriksson 100, 109
Alfa-Laval 19, 113, 121, 126, 134, 140, 161, 172
AOD process 79
Ari AB 100
Arboga Maskiner 113
ASEA 35, 38–9, 47–82, 113, 126–7, 134, 159, 173
ASEA-Hafo 35
ASEA-SKF process 48, 68
ASEA-STORA process 49–67, 78, 80
ASEA Nyby process 49, 66–78
Atlas Copco 8, 113, 134, 157, 161, 164, 173
atmosphere 9
atomization 49–60, 65, 67–73
automatic production 102
automization 105, 114
automobile 32, 38–9, 76
   industry 50, 78, 94
Avesta 46, 141

Bahco AB 93
ball bearings 45
Bell Laboratories 29
bench drilling 112
BFI 47
BMW 78–9
Bofors 41, 46, 146
break-down 106
Britool 94
broaches 49
Bröderna Lindqvist 100
Buhrmeister & Wein 126
Bulten AB 93
business analysis 85

CAD 30
CAE 30
CAM 30

225

226

Author Index

Abernathy, W.J., 26, 31, 87, 92
Aldrich, H.E., 8, 25, 171
Allen T.J., 178
Avlonitis, G.J., 31
Axelsson, B., 33, 63, 86, 133, 170, 171
Axelsson, H., 126

Baranson, J., 37, 87
Belshaw, C.S., 219
Bengtsson, W., 48
Bergqvist, S., 186
Björk, L., 126
Blau, P., 170
Blois, K.J., 31
Brunsson, N., 125
Carlson, S., 126
Carlsson, B., 28, 125
Cook, K.S., 14, 209
Cunningham, M.T., 126, 177
Czepiel, J.A., 178
Dahl, R.A., 171
Dahmén, E., 28, 125
Edvall, Å., 126
Emerson, R.M., 14, 209
Emmit, D.G., 8
Epstein, E.M., 25
Evan, W.M., 216

Ford, D.I., 171,

Galbraith, J.K., 172
Glete, J., 82
Gold, B., 84
Golding, I., 85
Goldman, K., 172
Granovetter, M.S., 151, 209, 215
Grufman, A., 28, 125

Hägg, I., 14, 126, 171
Håkansson, H., 8, 14, 17, 29, 33, 43, 63, 82, 86, 126, 160, 170, 171
Hallén, L., 10
Hamfelt, C., 186
Hammarkvist, K-O., 14
Hedberg, B., 126
Hirschman, A.O., 10

Johanson, J., 14, 17, 126, 163, 170, 171
Josephsson, M., 28, 125

233

For Product Safety Concerns and Information please contact our EU
representative GPSR@taylorandfrancis.com Taylor & Francis Verlag GmbH,
Kaufingerstraße 24, 80331 München, Germany

Printed and bound by CPI Group (UK) Ltd, Croydon, CR0 4YY
08/05/2025
01864494-0001